Journey
to
Freedom

Journey to Freedom

Discovering the God of Deliverance

An Exodus Bible Study

NATASHA SISTRUNK ROBINSON

Our Daily Bread
Publishing™

Journey to Freedom: Discovering the God of Deliverance, An Exodus Bible Study
© 2022 by Natasha Sistrunk Robinson

Interior design by Darren Welch Design

ISBN: 978-1-64070-161-8

Library of Congress Cataloging-in-Publication Data Available

Printed in the United States of America
22 23 24 25 26 27 28 29 / 8 7 6 5 4 3 2 1

For our patriarch
Walker Amaker, Sr.
April 16, 1925–December 30, 2021
I'll see you at the gate, I know.

Contents

Introduction

When I attended college, the woman who discipled me and taught me how to study the Bible regularly said, "The Bible is God's story." The Bible is God's story, and therefore it is a gift, truth, and guide for God's people. I love the Bible because it is God's inspired Word, informing us of who God is and what God has done. Taking that journey of exploration is what puts us all on the path of freedom. If we discover God, the Creator, then we discover ourselves as His created beings—both the good and righteousness that come from God, and the rebellion and pride that cause us to go our own way. We discover our unique purpose in God's story.

Exodus is one of the biblical stories that we visit regularly because the people of Israel remind us so much of ourselves. If we are honest, we can confess that we, too, are stiff-necked people who reject the grace, good order, and holy standards that God sets before us. Yet, He continues to woo us. He has promised to save and is intent to deliver us from our enemy and from ourselves. Thanks be to God the Father, for setting His redemption plan in motion.

Thank you for trusting me as your traveling companion on this journey to freedom. It has long been my desire to write a Bible study on Exodus that I could present as a layperson's commentary. I wanted to write a study that was theologically rich, historically accurate, socially conscious, and accessible to those who do not have the privilege of attending seminary. Remembering that the Bible is God's story, and we are God's people, provides context for how we enter the narrative of Exodus. We enter as observers of history, remembering that these are our ancestors. Some of us enter as New Testament believers, Christians, to understand the foundations of our faith and the hope that we have in Jesus Christ.

The Exodus narrative specifically has a rich history and tradition for African Americans, descendants of the Transatlantic Slave Trade. Harriet Tubman, conductor of the Underground Railroad, was often called "Moses" for delivering her people out of slavery. The songs, prayers, and stories of God's deliverance of formerly enslaved Africans has been carried by African Americans across generations. Perhaps this is the first time that you are reading a Bible study authored by an African American woman who carries this history of God's deliverance. My lens sees the glory of the holy God that has revealed His omnipotent power in the forms of smoke, fire, and thunder against the demons of darkness who seek to destroy souls; I look beyond the promised land to a beautiful city and a righteous King that is sure to come; and I interpret under the conviction of the Holy Spirit, who reveals all truth and is grieved by injustice.

My prayer is that you work through this study with a diverse community of people, that you take the time to reflect, complete the exercises, and answer the questions presented each week. I have written with the assumption that all God's people are ministers of the gospel, commissioned by God to become disciples of Jesus who make disciples of Jesus, and live as credible witnesses of the gospel of Jesus. Therefore, we have all been called to leadership. Together, we proclaim truth in the face of lies, shine light amid the darkness, advocate for justice in an unjust world, serve as agents of love to combat hatred. Taking the journey of freedom means that we live as people who know we are redeemed because we have someone that we are living for!

To this end, I pray that you bring your full self to this study and challenge yourself in the areas of leadership that are presented throughout. Then, commit to mentoring by sharing these words, history, theology, and truth with the next generation. Freedom of our entire being—the mind, body, and soul—individually and collectively as a people is the journey that we must continually pursue together generation after generation. Otherwise, the enemy of our souls will continue to lull us to sleep, particularly in the West, through self-centeredness, complacency, comforts, and platitudes of progress. But there is a word from the Lord: Be careful that you do not forget the one who satisfies you with food, allows you to build, enlarges your territory, and provides all your needs. Do not forget the Lord or let your proud heart declare that you have done all these things on your own. Instead, "Love the LORD your God with all your heart and with all your soul and with all your strength. These commandments that I [share with] you today are to be on your hearts. Impress them on your children. Talk about them when you sit at home and when you walk along the road, when you lie down and when you get up" (Deuteronomy 6:5–7). This is God's story, and we are a part of it. It's freedom time, y'all.

Remembering the Foundation of Formative Years

From one man he created all the nations throughout the whole earth. He decided beforehand when they should rise and fall, and he determined their boundaries. His purpose was for the nations to seek after God and perhaps feel their way toward him and find him—though he is not far from any one of us.

Acts 17:26–27 NLT

Commentary and History

SCRIPTURE READING
Exodus 1–4

Can I tell you a story?

I ask this question because we all approach the Bible in different ways, and because we all have preconceived notions concerning the discipline of Bible study. This is a Bible study about the book of Exodus, and it is so much more. The book of Exodus is a historic book, and most of it is written in narrative form. It is a story about a specific group of people, the Israelites. The Israelites had no concept of Christianity as we understand it today because Jesus had not yet been revealed as Messiah.

We begin by asking: what does this book teach us about God, as the original hearers understood Him from these sacred words, and His encounters with their ancestors through stories, miracles, and divine revelations?

The book of Exodus is first a Jewish story. It is a part of the first five books of the Hebrew Bible known as the Torah or "the teachings" of Jewish laws and practices. Exodus is the second book of the Old Testament in the biblical canon of Protestantism. Along with Genesis, Leviticus, Numbers, and Deuteronomy, Exodus is part of the Pentateuch (Greek name for the first five books of the Bible), which outlines God's relationship, law, and dealings with His chosen people. I mention these other books because the period of Exodus extends or overlaps with them. Therefore, we will read and reference these books throughout our study.

When I first learned how to study the Bible, I asked lots of questions. I still ask lots of questions, but the questions that I ask are different now. At twenty years old, I was a spiritual child asking basic questions which needed responses that could anchor me and help me make sense of my place in the world. As I continued to ask questions, I remember my mentor, Mary, reminding me often, "The Scriptures are God's story." Many years later when I attended seminary, I was able to contextualize that insight. I began to better understand and enjoy church history and watched intensely to see how God worked specifically through different individuals and groups of people

What does this book teach us about God, as the original hearers understood Him from these sacred words, and His encounters with their ancestors through stories, miracles, and divine revelations?

throughout history. I read a book titled *The Drama of Scripture: Finding Our Place in the Biblical Story* by Craig G. Bartholomew and Michael W. Goheen. That's when I came to understand that because of my relationship with God, the Bible is also my story. The history books in the Bible are a part of our global history as a human race, and we have been invited into God's redemptive story.

We know that Exodus is a story about the Israelites. We know that the Bible informs us of God's world and reveals God's redemptive story. And we are all a part of that history. We come to understand that the Bible generally, not exhaustively, also provides a theological foundation for understanding our personal history and story. From the days of cuddling with our parents watching our favorite cartoons, visiting Mr. Rogers's neighborhood, or hearing and learning our first words, we know that all great stories have a beginning and an ending. If we study literature, like I did in college, we also discover that stories typically have a setting, plot, conflict or climax, and resolution. So, with that foundational understanding, let's enter the story of Exodus.

The Setting

The Israelites are enslaved in Egypt, a country on the continent of what we now call Africa. The Israelites originally came from the land of Canaan, and they journeyed to Egypt as refugees to get food because of a seven-year famine that was in the land.

Make a note: The first character of importance is Joseph, whose story begins in Genesis 37. We will learn more about him, but for now, we acknowledge that the Israelites originally enjoyed peace and prosperity as a

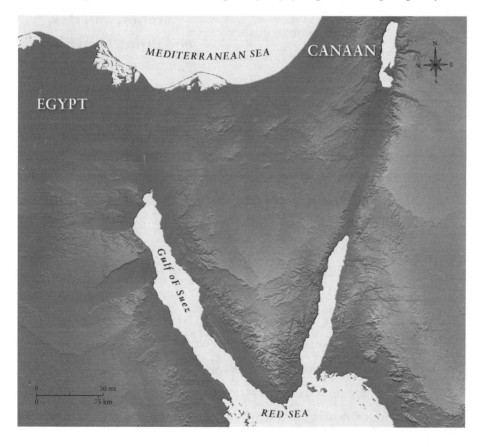

direct result of Joseph's favored position with the Egyptian king. However, Joseph's generation died out, and by the fourth generation, Exodus reveals that a "king arose over Egypt, who did not know Joseph" (1:8 NASB). The new leader of the nation did not know his own country's history, and that is the foundation of the plot and the source of the Israelites' conflict.

The Plot

Because all stories have a beginning, and since Exodus is the second book, we must know that the previous book of Genesis has something to offer which helps our interpretation.

We will begin our history lesson in Genesis, with God's call, promise, and covenant with a man named Abram. Abram set out for Canaan with his father, Terah (11:31). After his father died in Haran (v. 32), Abram became the head of household and continued the journey. God called him to leave his family and go to an unknown land (11:32–12:9). He arrived in Canaan with his family, including his barren wife, Sarai (11:29–31). After the move, God made a covenant with him which included promises (12:1–3):

1. Make Abram a great nation
2. Make Abram's name great and make him a blessing to others
3. Bless those who bless Abram, and curse those who curse Abram
4. Bless all people on the earth through Abram

Abram obeyed God without question. At age seventy-five, he packed up his family and his stuff, and made the move (12:4–5). This immigrant didn't question God. He didn't complain. He didn't delay. He just went. When he arrived in Canaan, God continued His promise:

Give Abram's offspring the land that he now inhabits (12:6–7, 15:18)

Abram journeyed to reside in Egypt because there was a severe famine in the land. After a while God spoke to Abram again, but this time he spoke through a vision. And this time Abram did ask God questions. *How could God's promise be fulfilled given the old age and barrenness of his wife?* God reaffirms his covenantal promise to Abram (Genesis 15).

> And Abram believed the LORD, and the LORD counted him
> as righteous because of his faith. (v. 6 NLT)

In Genesis 15:13–16, God gave Abram a revelation of what was to come. We see in the text that God is *not* simply making an isolated promise to Abram as an individual to bless his family. God also acknowledges this promise as a part of a larger plan which is intimately connected to and directly impacts other people. God is sending Abram's descendants as His vessels to bring about His righteous judgment on another group of people who are sinning or falling short of God's standards.

Questions

What promise(s) has God made to you in the early parts of your life?

Which ones have you seen come to pass?

What promises are you still waiting or trusting God to reveal in your life?

Day 2

A Family's History

SCRIPTURE READING
Exodus 1–2

God opened Abraham's wife's womb,[1] and she bore a son, Isaac (Genesis 17:15, 19, 21; 21:1). Isaac married Rebekah and they had twin sons, Esau and Jacob (25:20, 24).

The Plot Thickens

Jacob marries or has conjugal relationships with multiple women (that's another study for another day), including four women[2] who birthed twelve male children (Genesis 35:23–26).[3] The Bible is mainly concerned with these sons because they will become the twelve tribes of Israel,[4] conduits of the promise God made to Abram (vv. 10–12). Joseph is Israel's eleventh son, and the firstborn of his beloved wife Rachel. Although he is only mentioned briefly at the beginning of Exodus, he is critical for understanding the story.

---

1   God changed Abram's name to Abraham and Sarai's name to Sarah (Genesis 17:5, 15).
2   Sisters Leah and Rachel (Genesis 29:16–30), and their respective slaves, Zilpah (30:9–12) and Bilhah (30:3–4).
3   Leah bore Reuben, Simeon, Levi, Judah, and later Issachar and Zebulun (Genesis 29:31–35; 30:17–20). Bilhah bore Dan and Naphtali (30:4–8). Zilpah bore Gad and Asher (30:9–13), and Rachel bore Joseph (30:22–24; Joseph begat Ephraim and Manasseh, who were both claimed by Jacob in Genesis 48:5–6) and later Benjamin (35:16–19).
4   God changed Jacob's name to Israel (Genesis 32:28).

From our vantage point, dropping Joseph's name into the Exodus story is like the moment in an action movie when a seemingly insignificant character makes a power move, or when the underdog makes a grand gesture in a romantic comedy, or like having a mysterious character murdered during the first ten minutes of a horror film but you don't know why. Each action can shift story dynamics. If you follow the story line, you later realize the significance of the action or role the character plays in the overall story. Therefore, we must ask questions: *Why is Joseph a significant character? And why was Joseph in Egypt in the first place?*

Joseph was the dreamer among the youngest of the clan. He was also his father's favorite. His brothers were jealous of him and sold him into slavery. Joseph was a victim of human trafficking, and that's how he got transported to Egypt (Genesis 37). Eventually, his gift of interpreting dreams caused him to gain prominence in Egypt (Genesis 40–41).

When God gave Pharaoh prophetic dreams revealing seven years of plentiful harvest followed by seven years of famine, Joseph alone provided Pharaoh with the right interpretation (41:28–32). As a result, Pharaoh made Joseph his second-in-command in all of Egypt, a steward of the harvest and drought. Joseph married, had two sons, and made his new life as a trusted and respected leader in Egypt.

Eventually, the famine became so severe that people were flocking to Egypt from other lands to obtain food. This is how the rest of Joseph's family, Israel's offspring, came to reside in Egypt (Exodus 1:1–5), where his beloved father, Jacob, remained until his death (Genesis 42–46, 49). Not sure of their protection or the true extent of Joseph's forgiveness, his brothers were concerned about their relationship with Joseph and how he might yield his power against them given their father's death. In response to their concerns, Joseph replied:

> As for you, you meant evil against me, but God meant it
> for good in order to bring about this present result, to keep
> many people alive. (Genesis 50:20 NASB)

Although his brothers intended to do him harm, the bigger story reveals that God sent Joseph to Egypt to save them all. God keeps His promises. So, Joseph remained in Egypt and cared for his father's family until his death. Before dying, he reminded his brothers, "God will visit you and bring you up out of this land to the land that he swore to Abraham, to Isaac, and to Jacob" (v. 24 ESV). God's promise and covenant continue across generations and throughout history. "The people of Israel were fruitful and increased greatly; they multiplied and grew exceedingly strong, so that the land was filled with them" (Exodus 1:7 ESV).

All in the Family

SUGGESTED READING
Genesis 34

"Now a man [Amram] from the house of Levi went and took as his wife a Levite woman.[5] The woman conceived and bore a son" (Exodus 2:1–2 ESV). On both of their parents' sides, Moses, his older brother, Aaron, and his older sister, Miriam, are descendants of Levi, Jacob's third son by his first wife, Leah. Our family lineage shapes our identities and informs who we are. This does not mean that we must succumb to the old sayings of being "just like our mother or father." However, it does mean that our nuclear family and people that directly influence them have a direct impact on the ways that we think. Sociology and psychology inform us that for good or bad, our families shape our worldview, our subconscious understandings of right and wrong, and our implicit biases. History informs how we process that information, so being ignorant about our history stunts our personal growth, critical thinking, and decision-making skills. If we want to fully live in the present, lead well, and have influence in a diverse society of varying and changing worldviews, then we need

---

5   Jochebed is also Amram's aunt, his father's sister (Exodus 6:20).

to understand our personal familial history, the history of our faith, and explore how that knowledge can provide the foundation to draw us near to God, fulfill our life's purpose, and cultivate relationships of love with our human neighbors.

Moses is a descendant of Levi, and Levi was a hothead who was also motivated by justice. When his sister, Dinah, was raped in a foreign land, he devised a plot, along with his brother Simeon, to murder the perpetrator. Concerning the offender, the brothers asked their father a good question, "Should he treat our sister like a prostitute?" (Genesis 34:31 ESV). Their righteous anger gave way to rage and revenge. In addition to killing the perpetrator, they also killed the perpetrator's father and all the men in their city before taking their women, children, and animals, and plundering their houses. Sit with that for a moment. Because of our constant inundation of violence through social media and news cycles, it is so easy to read a story like this and stroll on to the next thing. After all, we also watch scenes like this for entertainment. As a practice of spiritual discipline, let's pause for a moment. Let it sink in that this is *not* a fictitious story or action movie. This is a historical event, a mass murder that is equivalent to something a soldier would experience on a battlefield, and even then, hopefully they wouldn't have children to contend with. Can you smell the stench of burning flesh and see the blood pouring from the male bodies? Can you hear the women wailing hysterically over them? Then can you envision those same women being pulled away, leaving the dead bodies of their beloved? There is no proper burial, only the memory of their homes dissolving into flames. And what about the traumatized children who would forever live without the presence and influence of the men in their families? Can you imagine the trepidation of these women and children carried off like prisoners of war with the same warriors who caused them such pain and suffering?

At the end of their lives, it was customary for fathers to bless their sons. From his death bed, Jacob said, "Simeon and Levi are brothers; weapons of violence are their swords. . . . Cursed be their anger, for it is fierce, and their wrath, for it is cruel!" (Genesis 49:5, 7 NRSV). This doesn't sound like much of a blessing to me. Many generations later, we will see how this rage bubbles over in Exodus, always resulting in violence. In more than twenty years of walking with the Lord, I have learned one thing: each of us are capable of the worst acts and yet God can use anybody. Any good thing that we do is only a result of God's goodness and grace. And any bad that is done, God can redeem. In Exodus, we will see how God can use a desire for justice and righteous anger, yet the Good Book offers a warning for each of us about this temptation and propensity toward violence. Moses's life and leadership are a testimony that God can use the good and bad in our lives and our familial history to shape and transform us as well.

Questions

What gifts or talents has God revealed to you in your formative years?

How have these gifts served you in adulthood?

What traumatizing familial experiences have impacted your family across generations?

What major family offenses have either caused blessings or harm to other groups of people, within or outside of your family?

The Historical Oppression of a People and a Blessed Hope

SCRIPTURE READING
Exodus 3

SCRIPTURE REVIEW
Exodus 1:1–14

Once Israel's family arrived in Egypt, they continued to increase in number just as God promised Abram. Their large number became a perceived threat to the new Pharaoh, particularly because he enslaved them and did not treat them well.

Pre-conflict

Pharaoh's command to deal shrewdly with the Israelites was strictly based on Pharaoh's perception and anticipation of their disloyalty or treason if war broke out (Exodus 1:10). During the time of their enslavement, the Israelites built at least two cities for Pharaoh (v. 11). Both the labor and the harsh treatment were commanded by the empire for the Israelites' only "crime," their existence. They were punished simply for *being* human and "other." This punishment began with their enslavement and continued with the genocide of an entire generation of their sons (v. 22). This is the regime, culture, and society that Moses was born into, and this is what prompted the Israelites to cry out to God for deliverance.

As an African American woman, born in the South, I understand the persistence of a people who are intent to survive in the face of their oppression and enslavement. I understand the tension, helplessness, and hope of those whose primary power and agency is exercised through prayer generation after generation. I know the slave songs: "Go down, Moses, way down to Egypt land. Tell old Pharaoh to let my people go." I know the Black voices who were led by the Spirit, like that of Mahalia Jackson, reminding a people: "Soon we'll be done with the troubles of the world, I'm going home to live with God." And lyrics like the Civil Rights classic: "We shall overcome someday . . ."

I am reminded daily of the racial traumatization that enslavement has on the shape of a people group. Students of history and social structures will understand that slavery is a systemic injustice that has continued to evolve for Black people in America. While generations of Black people were born into and died in slavery, most of their initial survivors were uneducated and did not receive reparations, and their primary source of survival was sharecropping or domestic work. They, too, cried out to God. Through Jim Crow segregation and lynching, they cried out. Through voter suppression, gerrymandering, Black codes, housing and education discrimination, they cried out. Through the war on drugs, mass incarceration, and police brutality, they cried out. They sung, they prayed, they lamented, and much like the Israelites, their prayers were heard by God. God hears our prayers still. The Bible records that the prayers of the saints are stored and received by God like incense (Revelation 5:8). And even though it does not always happen within our desired time frame, we stand on the truth that God is just, and He will break the yokes of oppression.

God sees everything and He is concerned about oppressed people. Just look at the evidence in Exodus 3:7–10.

Never discount the power of prayer, or think that God does not see, hear, or care about the things that concern your broken heart. Surely God sees. He is not so far away that your cries cannot reach Him. At the opportune time, God will come through with an answer. In Israel's case, deliverance came through Moses. Many years later, salvation came to the entire world through Jesus, Immanuel, meaning "God is with us." Because the Bible is God's story and ours, we have the record of those who responded in faith in the face of oppression and suffering. The writer of Hebrews records a "hall of faith" when reminding us about Abel, Enoch, Noah, Abraham and Sarah, Isaac, Jacob, Joseph, Moses's parents, and Moses. "These all died in faith, not having received the things promised, but having seen them and greeted them from afar, and having acknowledged that they were strangers and exiles on the earth" (11:13 ESV).

Oppression and suffering challenge our faith, and when our faith is tested, it is easy to lose hope. "Now faith is confidence in what we hope for and assurance about what we do not see" (v. 1). Oppression and suffering remind us of the fallenness of humankind and the frailty of our existence. Yet, these standard-bearers of faith remind us that God is still at work, and it is God's choice to use fallen, broken humans to accomplish His good will on the earth. Lest you think God is looking for superheroes, He is not. Yes, we know the names of Joseph and Moses now, but few outside of their immediate communities knew their names when God initially called them. God knew their names and when He called, they answered. Every day, God is calling ordinary people like you to stand in that gap for oppressed people. This is ministry, the work of parenting, being an excellent teacher, nurse, artist, innovator, business-person, community servant, or volunteer. It is the faithful work of the women who pray in the late-night or early-morning hours, or the men who stay with their families, earn an honest living, or consistently pay their child support on time. These simple acts of obedience may not get your name in lights, but God has the books, and you will be listed in someone's hall of faith.

Question

What are the names of the faithful people who are in your hall of faith? What do these people have in common? How are they different?

Fighting for Life

SCRIPTURE READING
Exodus 2:11–25

SCRIPTURE REVIEW
Exodus 1:15–2:10

Moses and his community fought for his life, before he became a catalyst who fought for others.

The first to fight for him were faithful women. Before God called Moses, he called two Hebrew midwives. Pharaoh's first genocide plot required midwives to kill all the Hebrew boys at birth. "While Pharaoh thinks men pose a threat to his power, he overlooks the real threat: *God is using the women to set the scene for liberation.* Enslaved to patriarchal ideology, Pharaoh disregards the women's power and character."[6] "But the midwives feared God and did not do as the king of Egypt commanded them, but let the male children live" (Exodus 1:17 ESV). When questioned by the king, the midwives crafted a lie about the strength of Hebrew women and their ability to deliver without the assistance of a doula. This lie has been the source of Christian ethics debates, some which ignore the reality that "Scripture

---

6   Kat Armas, *Abuelita Faith: What Women on the Margins Teach Us about Wisdom, Persistence, and Strength* (Grand Rapids, MI: Brazos Press, 2021), 59.

includes many examples of desperate mothers [biological or not] . . . who had to make desperate decisions based on desperate circumstances."[7] The midwives were offering their lives and bodies as sacrifices in exchange for the lives and bodies of innocent children, as their civil disobedience could have been punishable by death. Their sacrifice saved Moses's life. It is a common belief that Moses is the author of the book of Exodus. By naming Shiphrah and Puah, Moses is honoring them in his "hall of faith." God also honored them by sparing their lives and giving them families (v. 21).

The first death threat was to destroy the Hebrew people "from within" at the hands of Hebrew midwives who were responsible as givers, not takers, of life. When that plot failed, Pharaoh continued his path of destruction and had all the Hebrew baby boys murdered anyway (v. 22). The second path of destruction came "from without," at the hands of the Egyptians who drowned the baby boys in the Nile River. Make no mistake, this was not simply a murderous plot. It was a narcissistic and terrorist act to control the Israelites through fear, and to remind them of Pharaoh's power over their lives. We have seen these tactics at work in the United States. It is the work of lynching, watching violent videos of police brutality on Black and Brown bodies, or the separation of families and the mistreatment of vulnerable children on the southern border. These are not isolated incidents of fallen humans, but rather intentional and strategic acts of destruction and violence by people in positions of power. In contrast, the midwives used their influence to inform our faith by encouraging us to obey God rather than those who invoke terror and abuse their political power or might. These women encourage us to willingly put our lives on the line for the sake of the most vulnerable. Yet, the plot to destroy male children continued.

In a patriarchal society, the physical and psychological impact of a people group losing an entire generation of male heirs can be crippling. But Moses's parents said, "Not so!" They did not fear the king

---

7   Armas, *Abuelita Faith*, 133.

(Hebrews 11:23). When Moses's mother, Jochebed, delivered her son, her faith motivated her to hide him for three months. When she could not hide him any longer, she crafted a plan to save his life. His older sister, Miriam, was a part of the plot. This baby was placed among the reeds along the bank of the Nile and was discovered by Pharaoh's daughter.

Instead of rejecting him because of his ethnicity or people group, and instead of obeying the unjust order of her father, the king, Pharaoh's daughter modeled the way of Jesus and welcomed this stranger. By rejecting her father's command, she abandoned the societal orders of family and kingdom loyalty. Her heart was filled with compassion as she reached across the social boundaries of ethnicity, gender, and class. The Bible does not mention her fear or concern of treason; Pharaoh's daughter simply responded with empathy. She took Moses into her home, raised him as her own, and provided him with her protection while he lived in the palace.

During his formative years when he was most vulnerable, faithful women exercised their leadership, strategic, and persuasive skills to save Moses's life. If they had not done so, Moses would have never become an adult to speak with God or serve as His agent to lead the Israelites out of captivity.

Leaving Home

Moses grew up in the Egyptian palace, but he was not one of "them." Like many People of Color in our modern day who have been invited to the table, he didn't have any power or decision-making authority. Although he was an adopted member of Pharaoh's family, he would never be an heir to Pharaoh's throne. He was always on the outside looking in. The Egyptians knew that he was a Hebrew, and he also identified as such (Exodus 2:11). As he grew into manhood, he became conscious of his own people's oppression. When he saw one of the enslaved Hebrew people being abused by an Egyptian taskmaster, the spirit of his ancestor Levi rose in him. Untamed anger and his desire for justice met as Moses murdered the Egyptian soldier and hid his body. Moses thought he was doing right by his people. Perhaps they would appreciate his help, no one would ever speak of it, or they would lie about it to provide him an alibi.

However, it only took a day for the news to spread. When Moses went out the next day, he observed two Hebrews fighting. "And he said to the man in the wrong, 'Why do you strike your companion?' He answered, 'Who made you a prince and a judge over us? Do you mean to kill me as you killed the Egyptian?'" (vv. 13–14 ESV). There are many layers in this brief exchange. Moses cared about his *own* people, and that is why he inserted himself into both situations. That's what motivated him to ask the question of the "brotha" in the wrong. But there were some things in his young twenty-something-year-old life that Moses did not understand. While his affections were toward his people, to them, or at least to this brotha, Moses had become a "they." Moses was the house Negro, the one under the plantation owner's thumb, invited into his family, enjoying his pleasantries for a season, and who didn't have to suffer in the fields like the rest of them; and therefore, Moses could not be trusted. *You have no right to speak to me about something you haven't experienced and don't understand.*

Then the piercing question comes, "Who made you a prince and a judge over us?" Here's my Black woman translation: "You may have all the nice clothes and live in the nice house, but you ain't no betta than us. We may be fighting each other, but didn't you just murder a guy? You are just like your adopted granddaddy and our oppressor, Pharaoh. Sit down!" There is an old gospel song by the Williams Brothers that says, "Sweep around your own front door before you try to sweep around mine." And that's just a biblical exposition of Jesus's teaching: "Why do you look at the speck that is in your brother's eye, but do not notice the log that is in your own eye? . . . You hypocrite, first take the log out of your own eye, and then you will see clearly to take the speck out of your brother's eye" (Matthew 7:3, 5 NASB). Moses was exposed. The Hebrews knew what he did, and so did Pharaoh. I suspect Pharaoh was always waiting in the wings to find a reason to kill Moses, and now he had one (Exodus 2:15). To save his own life, Moses fled to Midian.

Questions

What roles have women played in your life during your formative years?

How does that awareness impact your thoughts about womanhood and leadership?

What has your journey taught you about your motivations and your community?

Day 5

God's Plan

SCRIPTURE READING
Exodus 4

SCRIPTURE REVIEW
Exodus 2:16–4:31

Moses fled to Midian before Pharaoh's army could get to him. God saved his life yet again. There he married Zipporah, and their first son, Gershom, was born. In this ancient culture, names had meaning. That is why God changed Abram's name to Abraham, meaning "father of many,"[8] and Jacob's name to Israel.[9] Moses named his son Gershom, which sounds like the Hebrew word for "alien" or "sojourner." This naming is about Gershom, who Moses perceives as homeless, having been cut off from his Hebrew people and heritage.

This naming is also a reality and identity marker for Moses, whose life has been marked by restless wandering. From the time of his weaning from Jochebed's breast, he never lived among his own people. Initially, he took up residence in the Egyptian palace. He didn't have a choice in the

---

8 Abram also means "live to the east / of." Reference Genesis 17:5 and 15.
9 Jacob means "he grasps the heel," just as he did with his twin brother at birth (Genesis 25:26), or figuratively it means "he deceives." Israel means "he who struggles with God," just as he did when wrestling with an angel for a blessing (32:28; 35:10).

matter. Then he moved into another man's home in Midian. Yes, he had a family and was building a new life; however, a new family does not replace the family that he lost, and it doesn't remove the grief or trauma of not being able to say goodbye to loved ones. I imagine Moses worried endlessly about the welfare of Pharaoh's daughter, his parents, siblings, and other family members. As Moses rebuilt his life in Midian, the Hebrews continued to suffer under Pharaoh's rule. Pharaoh died, but Moses yet lived. While Moses tended to his shepherding duties, God spoke to him from a burning bush. It is a familiar text and I expound upon it in chapter 4 of my book *A Sojourner's Truth*, so I won't elaborate much more here, apart from making key observations:

Observation #1–The fact that the bush is burning and not burning up is a miracle. Throughout the Bible, God takes divine actions like this to reveal His presence and uniqueness, and to let witnesses know that He is near and at work. Moses looked at the bush and stood as a witness to God's divine presence and work.

Observation #2–Out of the burning bush, God called Moses by name (Exodus 3:4). We don't know the Hebrew name that Moses's biological parents gave him at birth, but we do know that Pharaoh's daughter called him Moses, meaning "draw out," because she drew him out of the water. By now we know that God is the chief agent who has been drawing Moses out and rescuing him again and again. For the first time in a holy space, God spoke to Moses directly and invited him to live up to his name. God is the one who will bring Moses out of the desert and propel him to become God's agent!

Observation #3–God revealed himself to Moses: "I am the God of your father, the God of Abraham, the God of Isaac and the God of Jacob" (v. 6). We do not know the full extent of Moses's relationship with his biological family while growing up in the Egyptian palace, but it appears that he had some interaction with his own people and family to have had such affections for them, and for God to reveal himself to Moses in this way. God would not have introduced himself like this if Moses didn't know who Abraham, Isaac, or Jacob were. In doing so, God is informing Moses of his own heritage and of God's receipts. God is saying, "I have good credit—a history, dialogue, and track record with your people." In naming Abraham, God is also linking Moses's destiny to the promise and covenant that God made with Abram.

Observation #4—God attached the community's problem to Moses's individual calling. The issue at hand is the oppression of the Hebrews. God knows all about it, and He is about to go to work in response to it. Moses is a key piece in God's strategy for addressing the systemic and generational oppression of His people. God is calling Moses to divine work. Moses answered the call. After receiving God's assurance of safety, Moses went back to Egypt with his wife and sons.

SCRIPTURE READING
Genesis 17:1–14

SCRIPTURE READING
Exodus 4:18–26

God told Moses to communicate a message to Pharaoh: "Israel is my firstborn son, and I say to you, 'Let my son go that he may serve me.' If you refuse to let him go, behold, I will kill your firstborn son" (Exodus 4:22–23 ESV). God is using the metaphor of family to inform Moses that He is in intimate relationship with Israel. They are His children and heirs.

Before Moses can deliver the message, there is a plot twist. God met Moses at an inn and was prepared to take his life! Why would God consider this act after giving Moses an assignment? The answer is found in his wife's action and words. Zipporah "took a flint and cut off her son's foreskin and touched Moses' feet with it and said, 'Surely you are a bridegroom of blood [referring to circumcision] to me!'" (v. 25 ESV). God spared Moses's life because of Zipporah's obedience. There is much scholarly debate about Zipporah's choice of language and her attitude when taking this action. The Bible doesn't give us enough information to draw conclusions about the latter. What we clearly observe is Moses's life being saved again by a woman. Zipporah was not a Hebrew, yet she acted in alignment with Moses's faith. Occurring on the eighth day after birth, male circumcision was a sign of the Abrahamic covenant (Genesis 17:9–14). Since Moses was hidden in his Hebrew home for the early part of his life, we can conclude that he was already circumcised. By circumcising Gershom, Zipporah was taking an act that Moses should have already taken as a descendant of Abraham.

Moses is in the trenches now. This work that God has called him to is dangerous. It could cost his life, and the lives of many others if he doesn't get it right. By not circumcising his son, Moses broke covenant with God. Moses is becoming a leader, and all great leaders must first learn how to follow. Before Moses speaks God's words to Pharaoh, he must first adopt them for himself. It is not enough for him to accept God's leadership call. Moses must also go about God's plan, in God's time, and in God's way. Moses needed to learn quickly: *If you don't honor God first, He has the power to put an end to everything.*

Questions

What was a major time in your life when you either neglected doing the right thing, or tried to do the right thing in the wrong way?

What did you learn from that experience?

Weekend Reflection

God Is with You

Moses is human like us, and that is why God accompanied his call with the assurances of God's victory, signs of God's presence, and provided the right people to help accomplish his mission and keep Moses on the correct path.

> Moses would be God's agent for accomplishing this work, but Moses was unsure about himself and this call. He had questions. He asked, "Who am I that I should go to Pharaoh and bring the Israelites out of Egypt?" (3:11).
>
> Then God reminded Moses of a few key truths regarding his purpose: "I will be with you" (3:12). Because I am sending you, I will finish the work.
>
> In spite of these truths, Moses still had doubts and questioned himself and God: "Suppose I go to the Israelites and say to them, 'The God of your fathers has sent me to you,' and they ask me, 'What is his name?' Then what shall I tell them?" (3:13).

"What if they do not believe me or listen to me and say, 'The LORD did not appear to you'?" (4:1).

"I have never been eloquent, neither in the past nor since you have spoken to your servant. I am slow of speech and tongue" (4:10).

"Pardon your servant, Lord. Please send someone else" (4:13).

But for every question, every doubt, and every obstacle, God had an answer. For every person who didn't believe, God showed himself as true. Moses would not fulfill his purpose in his own strength. The God of his ancestors—Abraham, Isaac, and Jacob—would be with him.

Natasha Sistrunk Robinson, *A Sojourner's Truth*

Exercise

As we conclude this lesson, let's reflect on the chapter's title together, "Remembering the Foundation of Formative Years," alongside the primary question of this chapter: What is God doing? This exercise is an opportunity to practice the spiritual discipline of remembering. Chart out the decades of your life in your journal or on a separate page. For each decade, write down one high point and one low point experienced during that period. Some people refer to these as mountaintops and valleys or rosebushes and thorns. After you have documented the experiences, spend a few moments answering this question for each decade: What was God doing? Perhaps you want to mark each decade, each high or low, with a symbol. Be creative. How is God speaking to you during this time?

Group Discussion

1. What doubts or fears do you have about the work or communal mission that God has called you to (Exodus 3:11)?

2. Think back on your exercise about the decades of your life; what evidence affirms God's presence at work in your life? Go back even further to reflect on your family history or ethnic origin: What miracles has God worked in the past to affirm your present reality (4:2–9)?

3. Who is in your village? What people has God put in your corner to help you reach your destiny, serve your community, and accomplish your work (vv. 14–15)?

4. What roles have these people played in your life? How have you served them well in the past (vv. 14–16)? Are these still the right people to keep on your life and faith journey?

5. Where might be your relationship, knowledge, or leadership gaps?

_____

_____

_____

_____

_____

_____

_____

_____

_____

_____

_____

_____

_____

_____

Knowing God
and Seeing God's Way

I am the Lord, *and there is no other;*
apart from me there is no God. I will strengthen you,
though you have not acknowledged me,
so that from the rising of the sun to the place of its setting
people may know there is none besides me.
I am the Lord, *and there is no other.*

Isaiah 45:5–6

Day 1

Commentary

When Moses returned to Egypt with his brother, Aaron, they gathered the elders of the Israelites. This may not seem like a big deal in Western culture where we often ignore, cast aside, or dishonor our elders, but in this ancient culture, the elders—both those who were advanced in years and, later, those who held the official title as religious leaders—were respected and their wisdom valued among the community. The elders offered clear direction for leadership. When I was in seminary, one of my professors often said, "So goes the leader, so goes the people." We will soon find that to become true. As Moses questions his leadership responsibility to serve the Hebrew people (Exodus 3:11; 5:22), we will do well to remember the critical question: *Who is leading the people?*

When "Aaron told [the elders] everything the LORD had said to Moses . . . they believed. And when they heard that the LORD was concerned about them and had seen their misery, they bowed down and worshiped" (4:30–31). Although the Israelites had a shared history with God, this is the first time in the fourth century of their enslavement where they are being encouraged with the truth: *the God of their ancestors still cared about them.* He was keeping a watchful eye and God was attentive to their struggle, so they bowed down to worship. They spoke to the political or governmental leaders of Egypt only after they spoke and worshipped with the leaders of Israel. They approached Pharaoh neither with their own words nor in their own strength.

Throughout the exchange between the religious leaders and the political oppressors of God's people, we continually find Moses and Aaron leaning into the conflict with some version of the phrase, "This is what the Lord says . . ." The first ask is not for freedom or the release of God's people. The first ask is for God's people to hold a festival in God's honor to worship Him in the desert. God's instructions were clear. All the Hebrew people, including the women and children, must go. Their animals must also accompany them on the journey because the people would not know what God required for a sacrifice until they reached their destination. The journey would take three days, and there would be a consequence, either through plagues or death, if the people disobeyed God's instruction.

Pharaoh didn't care about the God of the Hebrews. He was only concerned with what the enslaved Hebrews produced for him, so with a wave of his hand, he ordered them back to work. Pharaoh's initial question, "Who is the LORD [God of the Hebrews], that I should obey him?" (5:2), is a rhetorical one for it is not his desire to serve God. His real concern is economic: "Why are you taking the people away from their labor?" (5:4). Therefore, Pharaoh put a burden on the enslaved to make them work even harder. He neglected the provision of their supplies yet required them to produce the same amount of bricks. He was unwavering in his harsh punishment even as he crafted a narrative about the Hebrews being lazy. The Israelites were troubled, understanding that they had now fallen under Pharaoh's rebuke.

Before Moses returned to Pharaoh, he went to the Lord. "Then the LORD said to Moses, 'Now you will see what I will do to Pharaoh: Because of my mighty hand he will let [the Israelites] go . . . he will drive them out of his country" (6:1). God told Moses that the work he is called to will certainly come to pass. Moses will see God's might on display as God humbles this oppressive leader and the earthly kingdom Pharaoh has built for himself. Then God calls Moses again to remember his history, the covenants, and God's promises to the Hebrew people. The great "I Am" has spoken! God doesn't just promise deliverance and freedom; He promises intimate relationship and redemption.

> I will take you as my own people, and I will be your God.
> Then you will know that I am the LORD your God, who
> brought you out from under the yoke of the Egyptians. (6:7)

Moses went to assure the people with these words, but the Israelites were sorely discouraged.

Then God sent Moses back to Pharaoh to tell him everything that the Lord said. Moses again offered excuses about his lack of qualifications (6:12), but God gave him a different perspective. I see this lack of confidence when God's people want to abandon the godly work to which they have been called. It can be something as simple as volunteering at church, serving their community, speaking truth to their family, or raising their voice for justice. Their response to God is filled with "I can'ts" or "Please send somebody else." When the stakes are higher, instead of being honest—"God, I am afraid" or "I don't want to fail"—they shift the conversation to something vague like "What are we going to do?" or "It doesn't matter what I do" or "S/he is not going to listen to me anyway," instead of being obedient to the call of God.

Moses's story lets us know that it doesn't matter whether we feel ready or qualified; when God calls us to action, we must respond in obedience, even if we are unsure or lack confidence. We will certainly be uncomfortable when God calls us to a difficult or dangerous task. We might face resistance, lose family members or friends. We might feel ill-equipped. We might fail the popularity contest, be lied about, or be rejected by our own community. That's why we cannot measure our faithfulness to God or success in ministry by the praises and followings of fickle human beings. We cannot always trust our own feelings or our self-perceptions. We must allow God to provide us with the perspective that we need to do God's work, God's way. Pharaoh is not in charge of this situation, but if Moses only allows himself to see Pharaoh's title, power, and might, then he will always feel inferior. But there is a God, and in God's kingdom or God's economy, the first will be last and the last first (Matthew 20:16). God said, "I have made you like God to Pharaoh, and your brother Aaron will be your prophet" (Exodus 7:1). Godly leaders are always called to confront worldly leaders who have rejected God's way to build earthly kingdoms for themselves. We are always called to become prophetic witnesses and truth-tellers who declare, "This is what the Lord says . . ."

In the same way that God saw the misery of the Hebrews and heard their cries, God is going to put His hand on Egypt to bring about judgment for the injustices they have imposed. By His own judgment, God is going to make a distinction between the Egyptians and the Israelites. In doing so, He will reveal himself as the one and only true God to Pharaoh, the Egyptians, the Israelites, and all their leaders. They will all come to know that He is God alone, and besides Him there is no other (Isaiah 45:6).

Questions

How do you normally respond when God calls you to a difficult task?

Maybe you have a challenging or dangerous assignment right now. How is your dialogue with God and within yourself?

What insecurities might need confession?

In what areas might you need to trust God more?

Day 2

The Stories We Tell

SCRIPTURE READING
Exodus 5

From day 1 of week 1, you may recall that the Exodus story has multiple layers. It is Moses's personal story and the story of the Israelites' deliverance from slavery; it is a historical account about miraculous happenings in Egypt. It is a part of our Judeo-Christian history, and ultimately it is God's story. Some stories are true, and others are fictional. Although fairy tales and fables are made-up stories, those stories are different from narratives. Narratives are the stories that we tell about the story. True stories can provide us with facts, but narratives lay a track based on the story that the author wants to craft given their personal analysis of a situation. Narratives are the ways that we present and share our understanding of the facts. Narratives reveal our perspective and the lens through which we are observing a situation. Crafting narratives is an art form, a learned skill, and if we want to understand the power of narrative, all we need to do is spend half of our day watching one news station and the other half watching a different one that expresses conflicting views. You may observe that the reported facts are similar, but the narratives about those facts are completely different.

If we want to understand and follow the God of justice, then we need to discipline ourselves to know and love the truth. There is an African proverb that says, "Until the story of the hunt is told by the lion, the tale of the hunt will always glorify the hunter." C. S. Lewis follows the narrative of the Bible to reveal that there is a Lion who is always ready to tell the truth that glorifies himself, if we are willing to listen. This means that we must push through the narratives—the stories that the ruthless oppressor tells about the "other"—and get to the facts so we can become truth-tellers and freedom fighters to the glory of God!

When Moses and Aaron asked Pharaoh to allow the Hebrews to go and worship their God, Pharaoh ignored their request. He told the people to get back to work and he was harsher in their punishment. He required them to produce the same number of bricks without providing them with supplies. Then he crafted a false narrative about the Hebrews: "They are lazy; that is why they are crying out, 'Let us go and sacrifice to our God.' Make the work harder for the people so that they keep working and pay no attention to lies" (Exodus 5:8–9). The truth is: Pharaoh had enslaved the Israelites for four hundred years, without acknowledging the wisdom and leadership that Joseph offered which saved the entire country and its surrounding neighbors from seven years of famine. The truth is: Pharaoh's wealth is due, in large part, to the presence of the Hebrews in his land. The truth is: Pharaoh enslaved the Hebrews not because of any violence, observed character flaws, criminality, or treason they committed, but rather because of his own narcissism and insecurities.

> **If we want to understand and follow the God of justice, then we need to discipline ourselves to know and love the truth.**

The truth is: during the time of their enslavement, the Israelites built at least two cities for Pharaoh (1:11). Building cities is not what lazy people do! Working diligently to meet quotas without supplies is not slothful behavior. Yet, Pharaoh named the enslaved Hebrews "lazy people."

The power to name is no small endeavor. It is an important part of our responsibility as image bearers. Before the creation of woman, Adam named all the animals that God brought before him (Genesis 2:19–20). Through this process of observation and naming, we learn that Adam had no "suitable *ezer*"[1] (v. 20). That's when God made another human to become Adam's partner and a complement. God provided someone who was just like him, yet different. This human was unlike the rest of the animals that Adam named, for she was holy, also created in God's image, with the shared responsibility of exercising dominion on the earth. For this reason, she was called "woman" (v. 23) and Adam named her "Eve, because she would become the mother of all the living" (3:20).

It matters how we name other humans, for naming can either be creativity inspiring or detrimental to the human's psychological perception about themselves and about other humans. Naming either strikes the match that ignites a movement of violence, or it kindles the power of light that sets us all free. Naming provides us an opportunity to become truth-tellers in the face of generational lies, guilt, shame, and pain. Whether formal or informal, our names have meaning. They assign power and authority; they communicate a person's worth and affirm their dignity despite their caste or social location. Therefore, we must pay attention to how we name and allow others to name humans who are created in the image of God. We must also be willing to "name" or call out a lie when we hear it.

Where are the lies? Sometimes they are hard to uncover because deception and manipulation are the work of our common enemy, Satan. Lies are found among the smoke and mirrors; they distract from the facts, the truth, and the real issues at hand. We have seen this deception and the crafting of narratives at work throughout our history in the United States.

---

1   The Hebrew word *ezer* (pronounced *ay'zer* with a long *a* like the word *razor*) is insufficiently translated "helper" in English. This word is used twenty-one times throughout the Old Testament, and sixteen of those refer to God himself as an *ezer*, a help or military aid and warrior on Israel's behalf. So instead of thinking "nanny" or "wife" when we see this word in Genesis, it is better to think of the woman as a strong power, force, or aid to the man, as they work to fulfill God's purpose and calling on earth.

Enslavement is a dark, evil, vicious sin that destroys the souls of the masters and slaves alike. It eats away at our humanity, the God-given image-bearing in all of us. It corrodes through the enemy's practices of lies, deceit, and theft which lead to destruction and death. To justify this wickedness, humans must craft narratives to dehumanize the "other," and set themselves apart from other humans whom they have decided to commodify and treat like animals. That's why enslavers ripped pages of freedom from the slave Bible, why US political documents have amendments and language like a "three-fifths compromise," why our US history books and education system are saturated with the narratives that some White men write about other people groups, and why the United States went to war with herself.

The United States and many countries around the world remain divided among racial, ethnic, and socioeconomic classes or caste systems. In the United States, these practices were first planted through the seeds of deceit, theft, and genocide of the Indigenous people—the original stewards of the land—and then watered and cultivated through the enslavement of Africans who were brought here to work the land. Instead of addressing the impact of this history and social analysis to provide restitution for our country's original sin, the colonizers—whose descendants continue in positions of power, politics, and privilege—have either murdered or cast aside the Indigenous people, literally hiding them away on reservations where many are suffering from the generational trauma of this bondage. Colonizers use that same power to craft narratives about the generations of Africans who have become African Americans, descendants of the Transatlantic Slave Trade in the United States.

We observe it when our government declares a "war on drugs" that targets Black citizens but labels the opioid epidemic a health crisis because the affected population is mostly White citizens. We come to understand it when our country welcomes "aliens of extraordinary abilities" from some countries, while labeling immigrants from other countries "murderers" or "traffickers." We see it at work when Black people are labeled "thugs" or Black kids are called "super predators." We are expected to overlook the fact that the US government provides "free" money to American citizens for all sorts of reasons, but for some people groups and at some times, the received money is called "subsidies" or "stimulus checks" and for others it is called "welfare."

In our state of postmodernity and relativism, some people don't consider the relevance of facts anymore. In recent years, our political leaders have crafted narratives with new language like "fake news" and "alternative facts." False narratives are *not* the true story; they are what the oppressor strategically crafts about the story to rationalize their own unjust actions. False narratives defend the oppressor's bad behavior while distracting citizens from confronting the real issues of injustice against the oppressed. False narratives reveal a certain point of view, and they can be dangerous, causing great harm to people created in the image of God. The real issue in this biblical story is: Pharaoh enslaved thousands of Israelites for hundreds of years, and it was a violent and oppressive practice. The Hebrews prayed, God heard their prayers, and God was about to do something about it. That's the redemptive truth.

Several biblical scholars try desperately to distinguish the enslavement observed in the Bible from what we know about the Transatlantic Slave Trade, because those of us who have studied the latter understand that there is no escaping the violence. Some students of the Bible prefer to talk about Old and New Testament slavery as "servanthood" or indentured servitude (because of our English translations). They want to inform us that slavery was a form of income, a means of work, and that some people sold themselves or their family members into slavery. I've been a student of the Bible and an anti–human trafficking advocate for many years. I also have living family members and dear loved ones who formerly worked as indentured servants, and I can assure you that none of these nuances (some of which are true) take away from the fact that slavery requires a power dynamic—often enforced through control and fear—where one human is playing god by owning and ruling over another human. Because all humans are image bearers of God with dignity, self-agency, and choice, maintaining human power over another human always requires the use of violence, and that was never God's original intent for His human creation. This violence is a direct result of the fall (Genesis 3). Before we discuss God's judgment on Egypt, we cannot ignore the sin and trauma of violence.

Moses fled Egypt the first time because of his response to this violence (Exodus 2:11–12). He saw an Egyptian beating a Hebrew slave so severely that he felt justified in murdering the offender. The day after that, he observed two Hebrew slaves fighting. Violence is traumatizing, and psychologists know that trauma when enforced systemically wears at the souls of individuals, causing personal trauma. It also causes a weathering or erosion of entire people groups leading to historical, transgenerational, physical, and vicarious trauma.[2] Hurt people hurt people. The violence and trauma that was imposed upon the enslaved Hebrews was also destroying them from within. The slaves were modeling the behavior of their oppressor, so violence was a regular occurrence in their lives. The gravity of the sin of human enslavement is detestable to God, and that's why God didn't turn a deaf ear when the Hebrews cried out. This biblical story reveals a true narrative that "the wages of sin is death" (Romans 6:23).

Questions

What stories have you told or what narratives have you believed about people who are different from you?

How do you discern if a narrative is based in truth?

---

2   Sheila Wise Rowe, *Healing Racial Trauma: The Road to Resilience* (Downers Grove, IL: InterVarsity Press, 2020), 10–14.

Day 3

Who Is God?

SCRIPTURE READING
Genesis 42–46 (Highlighting 46:31–34)

SCRIPTURE REVIEW
Exodus 6:1–11:10

At this point in the journey, Moses is eighty years old and his older brother, Aaron, is eighty-three (Exodus 7:7). Chapter 6:14–27 interrupts the story with their genealogies, beginning with the sons of Jacob (Israel), while focusing on the lineage of Levi. This is a reminder that our family history matters, and particularly that having a family history of faith in the face of adversity is critically important when we are entering a spiritual battle of miraculous proportions. Moses and Aaron will soon learn that the God of their ancestors will also be faithful to them.

God is preparing them for spiritual battle, telling them repeatedly that "I am the Lord." He is the God who established covenant with their ancestors (6:2, 4), and He has not forgotten this covenant (v. 5). Contrary to Egyptian belief, Pharaoh is no god at all. The one and only true God will bring the Hebrews out from under the burdens of Egypt and deliver them from slavery (vv. 6–7). This God will redeem them, deliver them by the strength of His own power and the righteousness of His own judgment

(v. 6). He will enter into relationship with the Israelites, make them His own people, and give them the land that He promised to their father, Abram (vv. 7–8). While the Israelites were traumatized and filled with unbelief (v. 9)—for the weight of enslavement can crush the human spirit—their condition did not change God's character or what God would do for them. It doesn't matter how they see themselves or what they are up against; God will keep His promises to His people!

We live in a fast-paced society. We expect instant gratification in all things from our entertainment to our meals. Too often, we don't want to invest, train, or prepare for the most important or difficult assignments in our lives—whether it's our faith, our education, or our relationships—because we are readily offered a distraction or alternative that will require less of us. The reality is: growing in our faith requires a level of belief in what we cannot see, and sometimes in what we do see but may not understand. It requires patience and diligence to seek the Lord, allow Him to reveal the truth of who He is, and allow that truth to become the most clear and guiding source of our *being* and *doing*. Maturing in our faith is not about how we feel or the circumstances or environments that we are in now. Faithfulness is about standing in agreement with who God says that He is and what He longs to do through you. If you cannot look beyond yourself and through your adversaries to see that, then I want you to take inventory of your life to record all the big and small ways that God has revealed to you, "I am the Lord."

What's in a Place?

Let's have a quick review of how the Israelites got to Egypt. Read Genesis 42–46. You will recall that Jacob's family arrived in Egypt from Canaan because they were trying to survive a severe famine. Except for Benjamin, Jacob sent ten of his "remaining" sons to Egypt to purchase grain, and upon their arrival, they encountered their brother Joseph, who was now Pharaoh's governor. Joseph recognized his brothers right away, but they did not know him. Joseph crafted a ruse to get his father and beloved brother Benjamin to come to Egypt.

When the brothers returned to Egypt a second time with Benjamin, Joseph revealed himself to them. During dinner, we learn that the Egyptians ate separately from Joseph and his brothers. You see, although they tolerated Joseph and benefited from his presence and skills, the Egyptians detested the Hebrews (43:32).

Over family dinner, Joseph delivered the statement, "God sent me ahead of you to ensure for *you* a remnant on the earth, and to keep *you* alive by a great deliverance. Now, therefore, it was not you who sent me here, but God; and He has made me a father to Pharaoh and lord of all his household, and ruler over all the land of Egypt" (45:7–8 NASB, emphasis added). God sent Joseph to a specific place to save his life and that of his family. In this way, Joseph went before Moses to embody God's deliverance and means of protection in the face of death, and in a place that was not his home.

When enslaved, Joseph suffered a little while, but the favor of the Lord was upon him, so he rose in wisdom and stature in Egypt. They were only two years into a seven-year famine. Therefore, Joseph was able to save his father and the rest of their family from certain death. Our history, legacy, and lineages matter to God.

Before Jacob headed to Egypt, God spoke to him in a vision to remove any fear of going to Egypt for God would make his name great in that place too (46:2–4). Upon their arrival, Jacob's family didn't settle in Egypt proper, but rather on the eastern part of the Nile delta in the place called Goshen. This location was close to Joseph, and the pasture was plentiful for their flocks, but they also settled in Goshen because shepherds were detestable to the Egyptians (46:33–47:6). By now, hopefully you are noticing two patterns: (1) God is the one who makes provision for His people in the face of death, and (2) Pharaoh will make concessions about who and what he accepts, so long as it benefits him. In Israel's history, Goshen becomes the place of God's protection and His provision. And when God brings judgment upon the Egyptians, Goshen will continue to serve that purpose.

When the plagues begin, we get clear descriptions of the destruction that comes upon Egypt, but throughout the account, we are also informed that the Israelites are protected in the place of Goshen which God provided. While Pharaoh originally put the Israelites in Goshen to segregate them, God's purpose was sparing the Israelites in that land, and He used their geographical location to make a distinction between Egypt's judgment and the grace He would pour on Israel.[3] In this place, God was proving himself as an *ezer* to Israel, and letting everyone know that it is the Lord who makes a distinction between Egypt and Israel.

Exercise

Ann Voskamp's book *One Thousand Gifts* became a *New York Times* best seller by encouraging readers in the discipline of thanksgiving, honoring the simple blessings of daily life. This is a good spiritual practice because we sometimes forget how the Lord has sustained us even through difficult moments. God brought you through the divorce, that deployment, the miscarriage, the loss of a dear friend, the rejection, the abuse, the lies, the grief, the depression. We sometimes forget that God is at work in our abilities. God made it possible for the degree, the certification, the job promotion, the opportunity that fell in your lap. God is the one who sustains the earth and protects us from dangers we cannot see. God is the reason that despite our abuse, the earth has not burned up yet. He is the reason that you didn't fall asleep at the wheel, weren't born at a different period in history, and did not crash in that plane. As a personal reflection, take time this week to record and give thanks for God's faithfulness to you over the years.

---

3   Exodus 8:22–23; 9:6–7, 26; 10:23.

When Kingdoms Fall

SCRIPTURE REVIEW
Exodus 7:14–11:10

SUPPLEMENTAL READING
Romans 9:14–24

We have entered the part of the story where God brings about ten plagues—each being more severe than the last—which lead to the humbling of Egypt. At center stage stands Moses as God's representative, who is using God's words to instruct a resistant Pharaoh. Their exchange goes back and forth with Moses asking for all the Hebrew people and their animals to go worship God, as Pharaoh wavers, bargains, and negotiates his position. The Bible speaks of times when God hardens Pharaoh's heart,[4] acknowledges when Pharaoh's heart was hardened,[5] and reveals occasions when Pharaoh hardened his own heart.[6] This reality causes much tension about God's sovereignty which is "the biblical concept of God's kingly, supreme rule and legal authority over the entire universe."[7]

---

4   Exodus 4:21; 7:3; 9:12; 10:1, 20, 27; and 11:10.
5   Exodus 7:13–14, 22; 8:19; 9:7, and 35.
6   Exodus 8:15, 32; and 9:34.
7   Stanley J. Grenz, David Guretzki, and Cherith Fee Nordling, *Pocket Dictionary of Theological Terms* (Downers Grove, IL: InterVarsity Press, 1999), 109.

The human argument goes something like: "If God made Pharaoh respond in this way, why is Pharaoh also blamed for his stubbornness? And more importantly, why are all of the Egyptian people suffering because of it?" The second question assumes that the Egyptian people are innocent, when they are not. They have all benefited from the Israelites' enslavement. This is what police and justice advocates mean when they say that an individual, community, or organization is "complicit" in a wrongdoing. Despite their guilt, there were times when God was merciful and compassionate to the Egyptians. God told them to stay inside with their animals when the hail was coming. Those who listened were spared, and those who didn't were not (Exodus 9:19–20).

In these passages, we see God finally providing deliverance for an enslaved people, so they have a hope and a future. But *what about the ones who didn't make it? What about the enslaved bodies that were overworked, undervalued, malnourished, violently assaulted, who lived and died in their enslavement for centuries? Who would give an account for all those human lives and dead bodies?* God was now demanding an account! After the eighth plague, it is telling that the Egyptian officials—when confronted with their own mortality—asked Pharaoh, "How long will you let [Moses] hold us hostage?" (10:7 NLT). After a few days of duress, they were asking their god the same questions that the Hebrews were asking *Yahweh.*

God was bringing this earthly kingdom to its knees, and they knew it. Therefore, they pleaded with their god, Pharaoh, "Let the [Hebrew] people go, so that they may worship the LORD their God. Do you not yet realize that Egypt is ruined?" (v. 7). The kingdom was falling and unfortunately the people were collateral damage. Let this serve as a warning to us all. The wages of sin is always death (Romans 6:23). While their kingdom looked great and carried on with business as usual on the outside, because of their refusal to repent of their systemic injustices and sin, their kingdom was inwardly corroding long before Moses showed up with these demands. However, their fall was only evident to them now that their sins were publicly named and confronted, and their leader was unwilling to change. In his book, *Building the Bridge as You Walk on It*, Robert E. Quinn wrote:

> Rather than accepting the need for deep change, most of us practice denial. We rationalize away the signals that call us to courage and growth. We work very hard to preserve our current ego or culture. To give them up is to give up control. Normally we work hard to avoid the surrender of control. Instead, we strive to stay in our zone of comfort and control. Given the choice between deep change or slow death, we tend to choose slow death.[8]

The Egyptians were comfortable because of the enslavement of the Hebrews, and Pharaoh's control of the people shaped the culture. Because of his refusal to submit to deep change, their Egyptian kingdom was all undergoing a slow death, so when Pharaoh's fate was sealed, theirs was sealed along with it. We must carefully choose what leaders to follow, and also commit to becoming the types of courageous leaders that will humbly submit to God and willingly change culture when God calls us to account.

So Goes the King, So Goes the Kingdom

The first plague of blood corrupts the Egyptian water source, the Nile River. It is followed by the plagues of frogs, gnats, and flies. The plagues of livestock and festering boils hurt their food supply and sources of earning, and attack the security of their military might. The plagues of the hailstorm and locusts destroy the beauty of their plant life and another source of food. The plague of darkness is a source of terror so thick that

---

8   Robert E. Quinn, *Building the Bridge as You Walk on It: A Guide For Leading Change* (San Francisco: Jossey-Bass, 2004), 6.

you could feel it. The people could not see each other for three days. Then came the death of the Egyptian firstborn humans and animals.

The destruction has come upon the kingdom, which brings us back to the first question, "Why is Pharaoh blamed for his stubbornness?" First-century Christian believers also wrestled with this question, and the apostle Paul provides his response in Romans 9:14–24. Paul wrote that although there are many mysteries about the world and the Divine that we do not understand, we can cling to these biblical truths:

1. God is just (v. 14); and
2. God has the authority to show mercy and compassion to whomever He chooses (vv. 15–16, 18).

Let's get real. God's judgment only seems harsh to people who think that sin is no big deal. We must not read history books or the Bible, pacifying the sin and violence observed, while ignoring the lengths God will exercise to correct them. God was merciful to Pharaoh and the Egyptians for the centuries they engaged in and benefited from the sins of slavery. Now was the time for God's judgment.

The apostle Paul wrote to tell Christians that Pharaoh is no special human. God is the creator of all things and all people, and God has the sovereign right to create different people for different purposes. The seventh plague arrived, and God had Moses explain to Pharaoh the seriousness of the situation. God revealed, "For by now I could have stretched out my hand and struck you and your people with a plague that would have wiped you off the earth. But I have raised you up for this very purpose, that I might show you my power and that my name might be proclaimed in all the earth" (Exodus 9:15–16). This cycle of negotiations is no negotiation at all.

On occasion, we have heard the president of the United States and military leaders say, "We do not negotiate with terrorists." Pharaoh is a terrorist, and God is not considering giving Pharaoh anything. God's purpose in this endeavor is to let Pharaoh and all the people know that Pharaoh is no god at all, and he doesn't have as much control as he thinks. God's intent is to humble Pharaoh (10:3) who has been playing god in the lives of the Hebrew *and* the Egyptian people. God could have slayed Pharaoh, but without this magnificent display, the people would have surely replaced him with another and carried on with business as usual. That's how social systems work. I've heard it said, "God didn't just want to get the Israelites out of Egypt, but God wanted to get Egypt out of them." The truth is that God was challenging all the watching eyes and listening ears to divest from Pharaoh what they thought they knew about him, his divinity, and his kingdom. Paul wrote that God did this so that His glory would be made known to both the Hebrews (Jews) and the Gentiles (those who do not identity as Jewish) (Romans 9:23–24). God is all powerful and no earthly, unjust kingdom will stand under the righteous judgment of God's mighty hand.

Question

Where do you sense God inviting you into deep change?

On Truth-Telling

SCRIPTURE READING
Exodus 11

SCRIPTURE MEDITATION
Deuteronomy 4:9

The Lord said to Moses, "Tell the [Hebrew] people that men and women alike are to ask their neighbors for articles of silver and gold" (Exodus 11:2). When reading Exodus 11:1–3, we see that God is a keeper of His promises. He is going to accomplish His good will on the earth. When God announces the last plague, He informs Moses that because of it Pharaoh will beg all the Israelites to leave Egypt with their animals and the rest of their stuff. But that's not all; God tells Moses that the Hebrews should ask the Egyptians for some of their wealth before departing. Because the Egyptians have seen the hand of God at work among them, they are going to grant this request. They are going to give the Israelites what they ask for. Why? Because God has changed their hearts concerning the Israelites. The Bible says that "the Lord made the Egyptians favorably disposed toward the people, and Moses himself was highly regarded in Egypt" (v. 3). You would have thought that after all the miraculous occurrences, perhaps the Egyptians would be angry, bitter, resentful, or even afraid, but not favorable. God was turning things around for good. This text provides a biblical foundation for why we need to tell the truth about reparations.

The Case for Reparations

Before Ta-Nehisi Coates published his *New York Times* best-selling book *Between the World and Me*, he authored *The Atlantic* essay titled "The Case for Reparations." Coates wrote, "Reparations—by which I mean the full acceptance of our collective biography and its consequences—is the price we must pay to see ourselves squarely. . . . [It is the thing that] beckons us to reject the intoxication of hubris and see America as it is—the work of fallible humans."[9] He began the article with the subheading, "Two hundred fifty years of slavery. Ninety years of Jim Crow. Sixty years of separate but equal [but not equal or equitable]. Thirty-five years of racist housing policy. Until we reckon with our compounding moral debts, America will never be whole,"[10] and he included the Scripture Deuteronomy 15:12–15. This passage put boundaries on the period of time that Hebrews could enslave other humans, and provided instruction for the liberal provisions that must be given so the newly freed person could make a life for his- or herself. The motivation for this generosity is because God required it, and because the Israelites were to remember with compassion the injustices of their former enslavement.

In the article, Coates wrote eloquently about the violence imposed on Black people, the lingering effects of slavery, and the history of how Blacks were cut out of the housing market and have been denied the opportunity to gain a financial inheritance or build wealth. Some people want to ignore or forget this history while they craft narratives to explain

---

9   Ta-Nehisi Coates, "The Case for Reparations," *The Atlantic*, June 2014, https://www.theatlantic.com/magazine/archive/2014/06/the-case-for-reparations/361631/.

10   Coates, "The Case for Reparations."

the ills that we see in some Black communities. Coates acknowledges this when writing:

> The laments about "black pathology," the criticism of black family structures by pundits and intellectuals, ring hollow in a country whose existence was predicated on the torture of black fathers, on the rape of black mothers, on the sale of black children. An honest assessment of America's relationship to the black family reveals the country to be not its nurturer but its destroyer.[11]

The narratives want us to ignore the original sins of this destruction and move forward. I am asking my neighbors *not* to overlook it. People are afraid to talk about reparations, partially because they don't understand it. *Merriam-Webster* simply defines *reparations* as "repairing," "the act of making amends . . . or giving satisfaction for a wrong or injury," or "payment of damages."[12] Most people who think about reparations only consider the latter definition. When we talk about making payment, other questions arise like, Will payment be made with my tax money? Who is going to pay? What must payers give up or lose, and what happens if the country is unable to pay? "The idea of reparations is frightening not simply because we might lack the ability to pay. The idea of reparations threatens something much deeper—America's heritage, history, and standing in the world."[13]

So why talk about reparations, and why now in a Bible study? Coates is motivated as a truth-teller, journalist, and humanitarian. I would also say that his writing is quite patriotic. He wrote, "An America that asks what it owes its most vulnerable citizens is improved and humane. An America that looks away is ignoring not just the sins of the past but the sins of the

---

11   Coates.
12   *Merriam-Webster*, s.v. "reparation (*n.*)," accessed December 3, 2021, https://www.merriam-webster.com/dictionary/reparations.
13   Coates, "The Case for Reparations."

present and the certain sins of the future."[14] I agree with him, and I'm also motivated by the definitions to "repair" and "make amends for a wrong or injury." I am motivated because reparations, my sisters and brothers, is a biblical concept. Not sending people away empty-handed when you have financially robbed them is an act of restitution, and that is what we see happening in the book of Exodus.

The Egyptians did not make an equitable payment, but when Christians think about faulty financial exchanges, we must know that restitution is a required act of reconciliation. We have a higher calling to repair what we have broken! The tax collector Zacchaeus understood and modeled this Christian behavior in Luke 19:1–10 when he paid back what he stole with interest. Restoration, peace, unity, and all the things that we pray to God for will never truly come to us as a collective people until we consistently tell the truth and make amends for the generational harm that has been done. We must ask the Lord to give us eyes to see, a humble heart to change, and the courage to repent and go in another direction.

Becoming Truth-Tellers

Truth-telling is an important Christian ethic, and throughout this Exodus journey we will come to learn that remembering is also an essential spiritual discipline. As I have written:

> The act of remembrance lets us know we are not alone in this world. God is present with us. When we remember God's presence, we better understand the history of our Christian family and heritage. We affirm our true identity and commitment to this family every time we read the Word of God to learn history from the patriarchs, prophets,

---

14 Coates.

kings, priests, and apostles; every time we cry out to Yahweh through prayers or songs of deliverance; every time we read a Christian biography or study the life of a hero or 'shero' of the faith; and every time we praise and listen intently to a testimony shared in our midst.[15]

Since you have chosen to engage God's Word with me, I consider us family. You are a neighbor who is being hosted at my table. Being intimately present with you as my authentic self requires my honesty, and my presence must also include the testimony about my people. Many African American Christians still believe the song "We've Come This Far by Faith." So, I will continue to remember my ancestors and tell the truth that African Americans have worked to exercise our dignity, nurture our communities, and build something out of nothing in a country that—although built by us—was not made for us. Throughout US history, exercising our human dignity to *be* free and *build* has been met legally, politically, and sometimes spiritually with White resistance.

At the time of my writing, the United States is commemorating the one hundredth anniversary of the Tulsa Massacre where White mobs terrorized and murdered three hundred Black people and left thousands of others homeless in one of the biggest attacks of racial violence in American history. Like the Israelites assigned to Goshen, nearly ten thousand African Americans made their home in the Black Greenwood neighborhood (also known as "Black Wall Street" for its Black entrepreneurship and innovation) of Tulsa, Oklahoma.

Like so many stories before and after it, the massacre began after a Black boy, Dick Rowland, was falsely accused of sexually assaulting a White woman. After his arrest, a White mob prepared to murder Rowland but they were restricted by the sheriff's office and a group

---

15   Natasha Sistrunk Robinson, *Mentor for Life: Finding Purpose through Intentional Discipleship* (Grand Rapids, MI: Zondervan, 2016), 173–74.

of armed Black men, many who were World War I veterans, from Greenwood. In retaliation, over an eighteen-hour period, between May 31 and June 1, 1921, an angry White mob looted, terrorized, and burned the city, destroying more than one thousand homes, as well as Black-owned businesses and their community school, hospital, churches, and hotels. For decades, few knew about this story.[16] Now, there are living testimonies,[17] books, museums,[18] and documentaries which better reveal the truth of the long-term effects of Black enslavement, Black trauma, and Black death.

When Black Christians say, "Black Lives Matter," we are not all speaking about the organization or the movement, about which there are mixed opinions within the Black community, but we are collectively making a prophetic statement that we choose to see ourselves and each other as God sees us in a country that does not always value our Black lives and Black bodies. We are saying that we know the history, the untold or overlooked stories of injustices made against our ancestors formerly and against us presently, and we do not believe the narratives that negatively shape the lives of our people. We are saying that we know God, and because we know God, we will stand like Moses to demand freedom and boldly say to anyone and any system that tries to keep us physically, mentally, emotionally, and spiritually enslaved to "let our people go."

16 "Tulsa Race Massacre," History.com, May 26, 2021, https://www.history.com/topics/roaring-twenties/tulsa-race-massacre.

17 Daniel Victor, "At 107, 106, and 100, Remaining Tulsa Massacre Survivors Plead for Justice," *New York Times*, June 1, 2021, https://www.nytimes.com/2021/05/20/us/tulsa-massacre-survivors.html.

18 "1921 Tulsa Race Massacre," Tulsa Historical Society and Museum, accessed December 3, 2021, https://www.tulsahistory.org/exhibit/1921-tulsa-race-massacre/.

Question

When preparing the disciples for His departure, Jesus left them with these words and a promise, "I have much more to say to you, more than you can now bear. But when he, the Spirit of truth, comes, he will guide you into all the truth" (John 16:12–13). Being disciples of Jesus requires a humility and deep longing and conviction for knowing, embracing, and embodying the truth, even when the truth is difficult to bear. This willingness and humble posture provide evidence that we are submitted to the work of the Holy Spirit. What actions will you take in faith now that you have been confronted with this truth?

God Knows the Truth

"Nobody knows the trouble I've seen. Nobody knows but Jesus." No matter how much people may deny, God knows the truth about history. That's the encouragement that we receive from Exodus. If we want to know God and see God's way, then we must also tell the truth about it.

God sent the Israelites a savior. By the time Moses brought the message of deliverance to Pharaoh, the Israelites had been in Egypt for 430 years. "God heard their groaning and he remembered his covenant with Abraham, with Isaac and with Jacob. So God looked on the Israelites and was concerned about them" (Exodus 2:24–25). Because of his concern, God sent Moses to deliver a clear message to Pharaoh: "Let my people go."

Can you hear the cries of God's people throughout history?

Through blood and white supremacy.
Let my people go.

Through frogs and slavery.
Let my people go.

Through gnats and black codes.
Let my people go.

Through flies and sharecropping.
Let my people go.

Through the death of livestock and lynching.
Let my people go.

Through boils and Jim Crow segregation.
Let my people go.

Through hail and voter suppression.
Let my people go.

Through locusts and racism.
Let my people go.

Through darkness and the war on drugs.
Let my people go.

Through death of your firstborn and mass incarceration.
Let my people go!

Slavery in all of its forms must cease!

Go down, Moses, way down to Egypt land.
Tell old Pharaoh, let my people go.

Natasha Sistrunk Robinson, *A Sojourner's Truth*

Group Discussion

1. What narratives have you believed about the greatness of your country? At what expense was that greatness attained?

2. In Acts 17:26, Paul wrote that God determines the exact time set for people, and the exact places where they will live. Where have you lived? What did God reveal to you about himself, history, and people in those places? How did those places shape you?

3. Reflecting on the African American history shared in this lesson, what insights have you gained from reading these historical accounts?

4. There might have been new language or vocabulary words introduced in this lesson. Which of these words, if any, would you like to discuss to gain insights and deepen your understanding with your group?

5. How has God revealed himself and His ways to you throughout the week, specifically by working through this lesson?

_____

_____

_____

_____

_____

_____

_____

_____

_____

_____

_____

_____

Celebrating the God of Generations

[The Lord] established a testimony in Jacob and
appointed a law in Israel, which he commanded
our fathers to teach to their children, that the next
generation might know them, the children yet unborn,
and arise and tell them to their children, so that
they should set their hope in God and not forget
the works of God, but keep his commandments;
and that they should not be like their fathers,
a stubborn and rebellious generation,
a generation whose heart was not steadfast,
whose spirit was not faithful to God.

Psalm 78:5–8 ESV

Day 1

Commentary

God spoke to Abram in a vision and said, "Know for certain that for four hundred years your descendants will be strangers in a country not their own and that they will be enslaved and mistreated there. But I will punish the nation they serve as slaves, and afterward they will come out with great possessions" (Genesis 15:13–14). God offers this word foretelling what will become of Abram's descendants in Egypt, while assuring Abram of the promises to come. "In the fourth generation your descendants will come back here, for the sin of the Amorites has not yet reached its full measure. . . . To your descendants I give this land, from the Wadi [river] of Egypt to the great river, the Euphrates" (Genesis 15:16, 18).[1] Our God is a God of generations; whether for good or evil, our actions can cause blessings or destruction throughout history and across generations.

The Exodus story reveals that thousands of named and unnamed people died because of Pharaoh's sin. Over centuries, even more died because of the Amorites' sin. On the contrary, countless nations would be blessed because "Abram believed the LORD, and [God] credited it to him as righteousness" (Genesis 15:6). You may think that you don't have much to offer; that you

---

1   Reference Exodus 13:5, 11–12.

are simply waking up, going to work, going to bed, and doing it all over again; that you fail as a parent; or that you are not the most competent employee. You may not preach like she does, sing like that tenor, or pray like the old church mother. You may not be the most creative or have the highest paying job, the best friends, nicest clothes, or the most social media followers. *But do you believe the God who has proven himself faithful across generations?* Belief is the act of faith that God wants to birth in Abram's descendants. When they get out from under Pharaoh's thumb, God immediately begins teaching His people how to trust Him and live faithful lives.

Chapter 12 is where the exodus takes place. The Israelites leave Egypt, but they do not leave empty-handed. They plunder the Egyptians just as God instructed, a small price to pay for

> **Do you believe the God who has proven himself faithful across generations?**

their four hundred years of enslavement (vv. 40–41). Six hundred thousand Israelite men left the kingdom of Egypt, and scholars estimate that the total number of the Israelite community, counting women and children, was approximately two million. The Israelites also did not leave alone. Other people groups left Egypt with them (v. 38).

As the Israelites began their exodus journey, God called them to celebrate first. *Look at what God has done!* This celebration is a seven-day festival known as the Feast of Unleavened Bread which is kicked off with the Passover meal. This feast and festival would become annual celebrations and memorials for the entire community to tell the story of God's righteous acts across generations. Through the book of Exodus, God provides specific purposes and instructions for each of the festivals and memorials the Israelites celebrate.

Here, God instructs Moses to consecrate every firstborn male within the community. In their ancient, patriarchal society, the firstborn sons were the heirs who received the primary inheritance and bore the responsibility of carrying on the family's legacy. That's why, in addition to grieving the loss of any beloved human, it was catastrophic for Egypt to lose their firstborn sons, and even more so for Pharaoh and the families that didn't have other sons. God is teaching the Israelites not to forget how he spared their first-born sons. "This is why I sacrifice to the LORD the first male offspring of every womb and redeem each of my firstborn sons" (13:15). Their firstborn males must now and *forever* be dedicated to God (vv. 11–13).

After the celebration, the Israelites journey to the land that God promised to Abram, but God did not take them through the Philistine country. This approach was both an act of God's grace and providence. The Philistines were fierce and fearless warriors. Astute Bible readers may remember the account from a much later period in Israel's history where one Philistine rendered Israel's king and his entire army impotent. One Philistine soldier had an entire armored and well-trained Israelite military unit and their king quaking with fear (1 Samuel 17). The Israelites did *not* leave Egypt as warriors. God knew that this group of formerly enslaved, unarmed, and untrained Israelites was not prepared to fight such a ferocious enemy, so out of concern for them, He sent them on a longer route toward the Red Sea (Sea of Reeds).

God guided them by a pillar of cloud during the day and a pillar of fire at night. At their departure, Moses—not Joseph's brothers—carried Joseph's bones out of Egypt (see Genesis 50:22–26). It appears that Jacob's descendants lived in peace in Egypt for approximately thirty years, passing down the stories of God, honoring Joseph's leadership, and recounting his desire to have his bones removed from Egypt. As generations of Israelites and their new community began their exodus, Pharaoh had a change of heart. He asked, "What have we done? We have let the Israelites go and have lost their services!" (Exodus 14:5). This is more than a statement about losing free labor, though the shift could cripple a kingdom that built its wealth on the backs of others. This statement is also about Pharaoh's identity.

You see, Moses publicly shamed Pharaoh, and God made a mockery of him in front of his subjects. Pharaoh is a king who is rightfully defined by his kingdom. He is no god at all, and if he cannot define himself by the rulership that he has over others, then where does his humanity, identity, and power lie? Within the social context of the United States, Ta-Nehisi Coates wrote about this "power of dominance and exclusion [as] central to the belief in being white and without it, 'white people' would cease to exist for want of reasons. . . . [And like Pharaoh,] the people who believe themselves to be white are obsessed with the politics of personal exoneration."[2] Apart from God, whether the kingdom of Egypt or the system of Whiteness, the human social structures of this world are defined by what actions they take over the named and mythicized "other" to maintain their own sense of identity, worth, and power. To that evil and darkness of this world, God says, "Know that I am the Lord." Whenever we are confronted with evil, we must know that God will get glory for himself! God is not simply crippling Pharaoh and his army; he is going to utterly destroy them! God wants Moses to tell the generations that God will fight for you and completely destroy your enemies, and He will do it in such a way that your enemies know that it was only God! When God delivers you, you must celebrate, you must tell your children all about it, and you must ensure that they tell the coming generations.

Questions

Describe a moment in your life when you felt an immense spiritual battle or physical attack from an enemy?

How did you get through the battle?

How did you experience God?

---

2   Ta-Nehisi Coates, *Between the World and Me* (New York: Spiegel & Grau, 2015), 42, 97.

Day 2

The Discipline of Celebration

SCRIPTURE READING
Exodus 12–13

On July 4, 1852, the formerly enslaved abolitionist Frederick Douglass gave his impassioned speech titled "What to the Slave Is the Fourth of July?" Like all great orators at a special event, he began by speaking about the purpose of the occasion. The Fourth of July celebrates the United States' political freedom from Great Britain. "This, to you, is what the Passover was to the emancipated people of God. It carries your minds back to the day, and to the act of your great deliverance; and to the signs, and to the wonders, associated with that act, and that day. This celebration also marks the beginnings of another year of your national life; and reminds you that the Republic of America is now 76 years old."[3] He spoke of the youthfulness of the nation, the history of the colonizers as British subjects, and their desire to rebel instead of living in bondage. But amid establishing a new nation, they became greedy oppressors, the very thing they despised,

---

3   Frederick Douglass, "What to the Slave Is the Fourth of July?," Teaching American History, accessed December 3, 2021, https://teachingamericanhistory.org/library/document/what-to-the-slave-is-the-fourth-of-july/. Originally published July 5, 1852.

for "oppression makes a wise man mad."[4] Nevertheless, they declared themselves independent and pursued their own freedom. "The freedom gained is yours; and you, therefore, may properly celebrate this anniversary."[5] But as a formerly enslaved person, Douglass needed to address the celebration with truth and integrity from the posture of the disinherited, and that is the same way that I must address this biblical text.

Douglass proceeded to recount the ways that Americans educate their children, the lies that are told from American pulpits, the exceptionalism that oozes from our legislative halls, and the narratives that are shared in American classrooms and at American dinner tables. *We are strong and we are great!* That is the narrative that patriots tell, these are the songs that we sing, and Douglass says that it is dangerous for a nation to continually perpetuate such narratives without owning up to the truth concerning her darkness. Instead of celebrating, he calls the president of the United States and his fellow citizens to wail, lament, and never forget the heavy chains, the bleeding children, and their sorrows. May we never forget AMERICAN SLAVERY, or reject the opportunity to see this country from the slave's point of view![6] Douglass beckons American citizens to tell the truth when saying, "The character and conduct of this nation never looked blacker to me than on this 4th of July! . . . America is false to the past, false to the present, and solemnly binds herself to be false to the future."[7] He speaks with boldness and clarity when stating:

> Standing with God and the crushed and bleeding slave on
> this occasion, I will, in the name of humanity which is out-
> raged, in the name of liberty which is fettered, in the name
> of the constitution and the Bible, which are disregarded and
> trampled upon, dare to call in question and to denounce,

---

4   Douglass, "What to the Slave Is the Fourth of July?"
5   Douglass.
6   Douglass.
7   Douglass.

with all the emphasis I can command, everything that serves to perpetuate slavery—the great sin and shame of America![8]

He continues:

> What, to the American slave, is your 4th of July? I answer: a day that reveals to him, more than all other days in the year, the gross injustice and cruelty to which he is constant victim. To him, your celebration is a sham; your boasted liberty, an unholy license; your national greatness, swelling vanity; your sounds of rejoicing are empty and heartless; your denunciations of tyrants, brass fronted impudence; your shouts of liberty and equality, hollow mockery; your prayers and hymns, your sermons and thanksgivings, with all your religious parade, and solemnity, are, to him, mere bombast, fraud, deception, impiety, and hypocrisy—a thin veil to cover up crimes which would disgrace a nation of savages. There is not a nation on the earth guilty of practices, more shocking and bloody, than are the people of these United States, at this very hour.[9]

Perhaps as Bible-believing people, we can use these national days of "celebration" to lament, wail, and tell the truth about America's history. We can formally rename, dissolve, or replace holidays like Columbus Day to include truth-telling, reparations, and celebrations that honor Indigenous people, the original keepers of the land.

Juneteenth

At the time of my writing on June 15, 2021, the United States Senate unanimously passed a bill to make Juneteenth a federal holiday. The

---

8 Douglass.
9 Douglass.

Juneteenth National Independence Day Act passed the House and President Joseph Biden signed it into law on June 17, 2021. The bill signing was met with mixed emotions for several reasons. Some American citizens had never heard of the Juneteenth celebration, and therefore the action had no real significance, and caused more questions than excitement. Other Americans continually expressed concern for the inability of the modern American government to work together on any bipartisan effort to make positive changes on behalf of the American workers and their families amid a global pandemic, political unrest, economic uncertainty, and racial injustice. Many Black people were especially concerned and confused because after years of increased racism and violence against Black bodies by the state, including the 2020 summer of global racial reckoning after George Floyd's murder by a police officer in Minneapolis, Minnesota, a federal holiday was not the act of justice requested. For centuries, Black people have asked America to remove all forms of slavery, not double down on slavery by any other name; Black people have asked for equal access and opportunities to thrive (i.e., housing, education, equitable pay, health care, nutritious foods, voting rights, etc.). Black people have asked for reparations, and for America to reconsider the ways that policing happens and for social services to be generously provided in traumatized Black communities.

Before it was a national holiday, Juneteenth (a combination of *June* and *nineteenth*, because that's what Black people do) was a celebration honoring the day, June 19, 1865, that slaves in Galveston Bay, Texas, finally received news nearly two and a half years after the Emancipation Proclamation of 1863 had taken effect. For some Black people, this day has always been an annual celebration, but for others it is new. Because we celebrate "Black joy" in other ways. This is what you need to understand about Black people: we know how to rejoice *in* our mourning, so we were going to do that anyway.[10] Much like Douglass, I suspect that Juneteenth should not be celebrated or reflected upon by all American citizens in the same way. I pray that it does not become another day off for mindless shopping where companies profit from Black caricatures, or where Black folks indulge in gluttonous activity. Instead, I hope that all Americans will take the opportunity to focus on our history, tell it to our children, support Black-owned businesses, elevate Black voices, and invest in the life and legacy of Black children, churches, historically Black colleges and universities (HBCUs), and in the health and sustainability of Black communities.

How to celebrate Juneteenth? I hope that Black people take the opportunity to rest, care for their own souls and bodies, tell stories about our liberation journey, and celebrate with those who love and affirm us. I also love the hopeful approach that Pastor Duke Kwon, coauthor of the book *Reparations: A Christian Call for Repentance and Repair*, posted on his social media account: "What if the period between June 19 & July 4 were to become an annual 16-day season of national remembrance, lament, and renewal—an honest accounting of the unfulfilled promise of liberty/equality, call to repentance, and recommitment to spur our nation to live up to its ideals."[11] I would add, "What if Black people did not bear the burden of that work? What if the people who have benefited the most from generations of Black enslavement bore the responsibility to prepare for such a remembrance prayerfully and thoughtfully? What healing might this preparation, annual truth-telling, spiritual practices, and services do for their own souls and for the healing of our nation?" I would love to see this vision become a practice across our country, but if not, we can intentionally practice this discipline of celebration within our own churches and communities.

---

10 Inspired by Lynae Bogues, "Happy Juneteenth," TikTok video, June 18, 2021, https://vm.tiktok.com/ZMdk5FFXP/.

11 Duke Kwon, "What if the period between June 19 & July 4 were to become an annual 16-day season of national remembrance," Twitter, June 17, 2021, https://twitter.com/dukekwondc/status/1405697967672250369.

The God of Celebration

God delivered the Israelites out of slavery, and they celebrated with the Passover meal and the Feast of Unleavened Bread. The Passover is a meal celebrated annually on the evening of the fourteenth day of the first month,[12] and it marks the beginning of the Feast of Unleavened Bread. It is symbolic, a time to remember the evening that God spared the lives of Israel's firstborn sons but destroyed the lives of the Egyptian firstborn in judgment. When the Israelites were obedient to God's command to place a lamb's blood across their doorframes and to keep all humans and animals inside those doors, the angel(s) of death *passed over* their dwelling places. The Passover meal included the careful preparation and eating of year-old, unblemished lamb. For Christians, this deliverance is a forthtelling of the salvation that Jesus—the Lamb of God—offers us through the sacrifice of His shed blood, which covers all our sins and spares us from God's righteous judgment. This annual feast also acknowledged the Israelites' future dedication of all their firstborn males, both humans and livestock, to the Lord.

The Passover kicked off the seven-day celebration called the Feast of Unleavened Bread. The Israelites left Egypt in haste, so "unleavened" refers to the bread that was taken which did not contain yeast. The celebration was a time of rest and included no work; the community spent the entire time preparing the meal, feasting and celebrating the goodness of God together. What a magnificent legacy for the generations to intentionally focus and learn of God's might and faithfulness to deliver their people from slavery. The purpose of the festival was to share God's legacy with the generations. "'When your children ask you, "What does this ceremony mean to you?" then tell them, "It is the Passover sacrifice to the LORD, who passed over the houses of the Israelites in Egypt and spared our homes

---

12   This is the Hebrew month Abib, the first month of spring (between March and April on the Gregorian calendar).

when he struck down the Egyptians."' Then the people bowed down and worshiped" (Exodus 12:26–27).

This festival was not for the Israelites alone, for God gave specific instructions for how the foreigners among them could participate in these community celebrations. In obedience to the Abrahamic covenant (Genesis 17:1–13), all male slaves, indentured servants, and foreigners among them could become circumcised—a blood covenant indicating their never-ending commitment to the Lord. Circumcision, like the celebration and the dedication of the first males in the community, is a reminder across generations and throughout history that these are people who belong to God! Therefore, the elders taught all the children in the community: The Lord brought us out of Egypt when Pharaoh refused to let us go. "This is why [we] sacrifice to the LORD the first male offspring of every womb and redeem each of [our] firstborn sons. And [this] will be like a sign on your hand and a symbol on your forehead that the LORD brought us out of Egypt with his mighty hand" (Exodus 13:15–16).

Questions

What annual celebrations do you set aside for your family and community to intentionally focus and celebrate the goodness of God?

How do you pass the truth of God's goodness and faithfulness on to the next generation?

Day 3

When Fear Invades

"We have let the Israelites go and have lost their services!" Pharaoh said (Exodus 14:5).

This old fox has returned to his same tricks, but God is still in control of the situation. God is giving Pharaoh license to pursue what his heart wants, which is to subject the Israelites to his power. But God has a purpose: "I will gain glory for myself through Pharaoh and all his army, and the Egyptians will know that I am the LORD" (v. 4). Pharaoh came with six hundred of his mighty chariots and stallions, and when the Israelites heard them coming from a way off, they trembled in fear and cried out to God.

They said to Moses, "Was it because there were no graves in Egypt that you brought us to the desert to die? What have you done to us by bringing us out of Egypt? Didn't we say to you in Egypt, 'Leave us alone; let us serve the Egyptians'? It would have been better for us to serve the Egyptians than to die in the desert!" (vv. 11–12). This is their trauma talking. Enslaved Africans in the United States were traumatized in the same way. After generations of enslavement, some of them spoke highly of their "good" masters and adopted coping mechanisms to stay in their masters' graces. Others could not imagine a life outside of their current condition, or perhaps they stayed on the plantation because of their fear or unwillingness to choose separation from their families. But there were many who did not wait for a savior, who aggressively tried to escape their bondage. Some of them like Nat Turner died because in a violent system, he responded in kind and risked his life for freedom. Others like Harriet Tubman, Sojourner Truth, and Frederick Douglass became abolitionists. Still others crafted songs of freedom and inspired Negro spirituals. Their faith overcame their fear with lyrics like "Before I'd be a slave, I'd be buried in my grave and go on to my Lord, and be free," or "Up above my head, I hear freedom in the air; there must be a God somewhere."

Don't be afraid! Stand up right where you are, and watch the deliverance of the Lord! As people of faith, we must be cautious when we are more comfortable in the sin, darkness, violence, destruction, or death that we know than we are willing to take risks that can open doors of new possibilities where God's favor and our obedience can bring light, peace, innovation, life, and a hopeful future. As for the Israelites, I imagine as sounds of the hoofs pounding the ground grew louder, the Egyptian troops rowdier, and as the sand dust clouded the air, their anxiety and heartbeats steadily increased and sweat poured down their brows. They must have wondered, "Is God playing some evil trick on us?"

Moses told the people to calm down. "Do not be afraid. Stand firm and you will see the deliverance the Lord will bring you today. The Egyptians you see today you will never see again. The Lord will fight for you; you need only to be still" (Exodus 14:13–14). Fear can paralyze us, make us irrational, cloud our thinking and judgment. It is a real emotion that can sometimes be a warning, which keeps us out of harm's way. At other times, fear is an emotion we can acknowledge even when there is no real threat. Either way, confronting our fears requires action. Apart from God, the Israelites are facing a real threat and they should be solely afraid, but with God, their threat is neutralized. God basically says to Moses,

"Stop crying! Consider what is in your hand and get the people moving!" Real people face earthly threats all the time. To that reality, the psalmist informs our theology:

> When the wicked advance against me
> > to devour me,
>
> it is my enemies and my foes
> > who will stumble and fall.
>
> Though an army besiege me,
> > my heart will not fear;
>
> though war break out against me,
> > even then I will be confident (Psalm 27:2–3).

Remember the tools God has given you to stand against the evil one.

Raise your staff in confidence, Moses! Why? Because God has promised, "The Egyptians will know that I am the LORD when I gain glory through Pharaoh, his chariots and his horsemen" (Exodus 14:18). The angel of God and the pillar of cloud moved behind the Israelites to create a barrier separating them from the Egyptians. When Moses raised up the staff, the waters of the Red Sea parted, and God—creator of the wind and the waves—held back those waters all night long as the Israelites walked through on dry land. God kept watch from the pillar of fire and cloud to cause confusion among the Egyptians. God fought for the Israelites as Moses lifted the staff in his hands again, and the waters swallowed up Pharaoh and the Egyptians in the Red Sea. None of the Egyptians survived. "And when the Israelites saw the mighty hand of the LORD displayed against the Egyptians, the people feared the LORD and put their trust in him and in Moses his servant" (v. 31).

Sing a Song

There are countless ways to teach important life and moral lessons to children. One of them is through storytelling, and there are numerous opportunities for our children to absorb stories. In addition to reading, I personally love watching movies and talking about those movies with others. In 2006, Warner Brothers released the movie *Happy Feet*, which begins with an elder penguin, Ms. Viola, teaching the younger penguins the most important lesson about being a penguin. During the class discussion, we learn the significance of a penguin's heart song. The heart song defines their identity as penguins, comes from within, and communicates who they truly are to others. Additionally, the heart song cannot be taught because the children must find it within themselves. But how do they find it? For starters, they are among a community of penguins who each have their own heart songs, and they sing together regularly. And in this classroom setting, Ms. Viola immediately calls the children to stillness, and then to practice and share their heart song. We can all be still, practice, and then share our hearts' song.

Songs have a way of speaking to our most intimate parts, and music can bring us together as a people. Songs like "To Be Young, Gifted, and Black" have power to shape a child's identity—defining the ways that they see themselves and their community. Songs can tell stories. Songs like Don McLean's "American Pie," Sam Cooke's "A Change Is Gonna Come," or "We Are the World"[13] define key moments in our American history. Songs allow us to worship God and inform the community about who God is and what God has done. That's what is happening in Exodus 15. Moses leads the Israelites in singing a song to God. This song will become their

---

13   "We Are the World" was inspired by Harry Belafonte, and composed by Lionel Richie and Michael Jackson, with Quincy Jones at the helm of production, and in collaboration with Stevie Wonder. In 1985, a total of forty-five headlining US artists gathered to complete the one-night recording on March 7 to provide funding to aid and provide support for an Ethiopian famine. Lionel Richie, "How Iconic Song, 'We Are the World,' Was Created," *CBS This Morning*, February 11, 2016, https://www.youtube.com/watch?v=vxMNLs7zryo.

testimony across generations. It affirms God's identity, praises Him for His miraculous work and the deliverance He accomplished, and makes praise personal for the people as they stand in awe:

> Who among the gods
>> is like you, LORD . . .
>> majestic in holiness,
>
> awesome in glory,
>> working wonders? (v. 11)

The people sing to declare that God has set himself apart from any other. Only "the LORD reigns for ever and ever" (v. 18).

Moses's sister and prophetess, Miriam, picks up her tambourine to lead the people, and takes the praise up a notch. The women follow her, and together they embody Psalm 30:11–12, declaring of God:

> You have turned my mourning into dancing;
>> you have taken off my sackcloth
>> and clothed me with joy,
>
> so that my soul may praise you and not be silent.
>> O LORD my God, I will give thanks to you
> forever. (NRSV)

As a refrain or maybe a chant, the women declare:

> Sing to the LORD,
>> for he is highly exalted.
>
> Both horse and driver
>> he has hurled into the sea. (Exodus 15:21)

This is how we are to respond when God does something miraculous.

The spiritual challenge we face in the West is that we have become so comfortable with God's blessings that we get offended and complain the few times things don't go our way. We don't praise God enough for the ways He consistently delivers and provides for us. Singing songs allows us to praise God for the present for what He has already done. Singing can affirm our backward-looking faith, while also providing hope concerning Israel's future (vv. 13, 17). Therefore, songs become the children's testimony: "[God's] mercy extends to those who fear him, from generation to generation" (Luke 1:50). So, we must always be ready and willing to sing a song. The group Earth, Wind & Fire tells us to sing a song when we feel down and out, when it's time to shout, when it's hard to care, and when a smile is hard to bear.[14] They inspire us to sing a heart song to bring us to believing, when we sense a loss in our lives, and especially when we have a need. We can always sing a song!

Reflection Exercise

In the method of your choosing, communicate a time when you were afraid or anxious. What thoughts were running through your mind? What did you feel? How did other people respond to the situation? Do any songs come to mind that helped you get through the experience? How was your faith activated or not? What did you learn about God and yourself from the experience?

---

14   Earth, Wind, & Fire, "Sing a Song," by Maurice White and Al McKay, November 1975, Columbia Records.

God Provides
for His People

SCRIPTURE REVIEW
Exodus 15:22–17:7

The Israelites leave the Red Sea and journey to the Desert of Shur. Then for three days, they were without water. Let's put ourselves in their shoes for a moment. Just on the heels of being delivered from Pharaoh's grip, they were mentally drained and emotionally exhausted. The community must have all been fatigued after traveling with children and animals, and being concerned for everyone's safe passage. Psychologists are familiar with Maslow's hierarchy of human needs. The foundation of Maslow's pyramid includes basic needs like food, water, clothing, sleep, and shelter. Maslow believed that physiological needs must be satisfied, at least in part, before humans can progress to higher-level growth needs like safety, belonging and love, esteem, and self-actualization. Additionally, the longer humans go without basic physiological needs, the more the deficiency motivates or drives their behavior.

I have never attended an Alcoholics Anonymous meeting, but I am familiar with one of the tools they use for self-awareness; the acronym HALT stands for hungry, angry, lonely, or tired. The idea is to take personal inventory to acknowledge these emotions and the dangers of making decisions when basic needs aren't met. These passages of Scripture confront the Israelites when they are most vulnerable and have been deprived of food, water, and rest. That's why they are bitter and complaining to Moses, but Moses acknowledges that their complaints are actually directed toward God.[15]

Being true to its name, the oasis water was too bitter to drink at Marah. When the people complained, Moses cried out to God, and God provided a piece of wood. When Moses threw the wood into the water, it became drinkable. The earlier part of this lesson was about God's protection. This section is about God's provision and a place. Marah is where God begins teaching the Israelites about their identity as His people.

Getting Egypt out of the People

Marah is the first place where God gives the people a conditional clause: "*If* you do this . . . *then* I will do that." God said, "*If* you will listen carefully to the voice of the LORD your God and do what is right in his sight, obeying his commands and keeping all his decrees, *then* I will not make you suffer any of the diseases I sent on the Egyptians; for I am the LORD who heals you" (Exodus 15:26 NLT, emphasis added). Before God provided the law or the Ten Commandments, He is already informing His people that the diseases the Egyptians suffered were God's judgment for their sin. Disease is *not* always the result of sin; however, what God is teaching them—and what the Israelites came to understand as reflected even in the New Testament—is a biblical principle, that the presence of disease *can be* a consequence of sin (see John 9). Sin offers up disease, but God is offering them healing through obedience.

One month after leaving Egypt, they arrive to the Desert of Sin, between Elim and Sinai. The people complain because they are *hangry*

---

15   The text acknowledges this on numerous occasions in this section: Exodus 16:7–9, 11.

(hungry and angry). And here again, their trauma speaks. The Israelites said, "If only we had died by the LORD's hand in Egypt! There we sat around pots of meat and ate all the food we wanted, but you have brought us out into this desert to starve this entire assembly to death" (Exodus 16:3). By now, y'all know the truth. This self-deceptive statement reveals much about the condition of the Israelites' heart. *The Israelites didn't just want to eat how the Egyptians ate, they also wanted to live how the Egyptians lived.* Their aspirations for life and "success" were defined by what the Egyptians did and had, so God has to change their expectations of what it means to live as *free* people submitted to a holy God.

God is their provider. *You want food? I got food. And you don't even have to work for it.* Throughout their wilderness experience, God is generous with His daily provisions. As He provides, He is training them to follow His instructions. We see the phrase return, "Then you will know that I am the LORD your God" (v. 12).[16] God is teaching the Israelites that He is trustworthy, and God is also making His relationship with them personal.

On that evening, God provided quail for meat, and the next morning, He provided manna, bread from heaven with its Hebrew translation meaning "What is it?" *For five days, gather only what your family needs that day.* We must learn to trust God with our daily provisions (Matthew 6:11, 25–34). This is their first test. Some of the people failed it. However, the Bible only records Moses being angry, not God (Exodus 16:20). On the sixth day, they were to gather enough for two days, so they could take a Sabbath day of rest on the seventh. Some did not obey those instructions either. That's when God asked, "How long will you refuse to keep my commands and my instructions?" (v. 28). Not only is God meeting their basic needs for water and food, He is generously meeting their need for rest. The Sabbath is a regular break they never experienced in Egypt! It is God's gift to them (Exodus 16:29–30; Mark 2:27).

---

16   Reference Genesis 17:7 and Exodus 6:7.

Water from a Rock

When I was growing up, the adults in my family used all kinds of sayings to let children know that life was not what we thought, and a lot of times, those conversations centered around financial provision. For example: If we asked to go to McDonald's, the response was a question, "Do you have McDonald's money?" In other words, whatever money the adults had wasn't going to support that clown. Another saying was "Money don't grow on trees." With this statement, our parents informed us that they worked hard to earn a living. They didn't walk outside to pluck money from a tree or to gather it from the ground like manna.

The phrase that regularly stumped me as a kid was "You can't squeeze blood out of a turnip." Turnips are root vegetables that cannot bleed, so what did they mean? They were aiming to communicate that you can't get something out of nothing. Simply put, they didn't have any money. I thought about these sayings as I reflected on the Israelites' journey from the Desert of Sin to Rephidim, where there was no water. They were complaining, but the water simply wasn't there. Moses asked them, "What do you want me to do?" Tensions rose as the community pondered, "Is the LORD among us or not?" (Exodus 17:7). Moses was so distraught and went to God because the people were about to stone him (v. 4). God told Moses to take some of the elders and use the staff in his hand to strike the rock. Water came out of the rock for the people to drink. Who can squeeze blood out of a turnip? Nobody but God!

Question

What opportunities can you take to share stories of God's provision with the next generation?

Day 5

The Lord
Is Our Banner

SCRIPTURE READING
Exodus 17:8–15

These Scriptures reveal that the Amalekites attacked the Israelites at Rephidim, but it doesn't tell us who the Amalekites are or why they attacked Israel. Their animosity was most likely a generational continuation of the twin rivalry of Jacob and Esau. The brothers fought from the time they were in their mother's womb. When their mother prayed, God informed her that the older brother would serve the younger (Genesis 25:19–26). Esau came out of the womb first. As a man, he elected to sell his birthright to Jacob for a measly bowl of lentil stew (vv. 27–34). Esau despised his birthright and his brother, Jacob, plotted (along with his mother) to deceive their father, Isaac, into giving Jacob, not Esau, his final blessing (Genesis 27). Esau's anger was so fierce that Jacob immediately left town for good. The brothers eventually reconciled, but they never lived in harmony (Genesis 32–33). Because this is an ancient culture of storytelling and oral history, we can rest assured that Esau's children and their children knew of Jacob's deceit, and perhaps harbored anger and bitterness in their hearts as a result. The Amalekites are descendants of

Esau, born of his grandson Amalek (36:12). It is possible that they spent generations waiting for the opportunity to get back at Jacob.

Remember that the Israelites were *not* warriors; that's why God spared them from a frontal attack with the Philistines. However, they will be required to fight for what God has promised, so they must get battle ready. This was their first training opportunity. Immediately, Moses commands a young man named Joshua to select a few men for battle. Then Moses tells Joshua, "Tomorrow I will stand on top of the hill with the staff of God in my hands" (Exodus 17:9). They didn't have time to get ready for the fight. God was reinforcing an important lesson when preparing for spiritual and physical battles: *trust God and use what's in your hand.* Finally, Moses delegated the task of assembling the army, but only Moses could reach for the staff!

Moses took his brother, Aaron, and another man, Hur, to journey with him up the hill. Whenever Moses held up the staff, the Israelites were winning. When Moses grew tired, Aaron and Hur put a stone under him to undergird him as they lifted his arms. Because of the support of these two men, Moses's hands remained steady, but what if he would have gone up that hill alone? What if Joshua was too fearful to fight, or was not obedient to select the men as Moses instructed? Victory for the Israelites was won because a few people trusted God and followed simple instructions to work together as a team.

"Then the LORD said to Moses, 'Write this on a scroll as something to be remembered and make sure that Joshua hears it, because I will completely blot out the name of Amalek from under heaven.' . . . 'The LORD will be at war against the Amalekites from generation to generation'" (vv. 14, 16). God is going to destroy generations of Amalek's descendants. God is also taking this opportunity to reaffirm His commitment to the Israelites across generations. Write it down. Tell Joshua. Remember what God has done for you on this day. "Moses built an altar and called it The LORD is my Banner" (v. 15).

Questions

What stories can you tell children about how God has shown up for you, your family, and community?

Are there rifts in your family that have been passed down across generations?

How has God prepared you to deal with toxic relationships?

Is there anyone that you need to confront or forgive, even if you cannot live in harmony or proximity to them?

Preparing Generations for What's New and Next

SCRIPTURE READING
Psalm 78

Our God is the God of generations. He is the one who fights our battles, and this is what we are to tell our children and the coming generations: *we celebrate the God of generations who goes before us to teach us and prepare the way for our spiritual battles, to engage our physical enemies, and to fight on our behalf!*

> Throughout the exodus narrative, God is teaching everyone a simple truth: he is God alone, and nothing else is worthy of worship. God speaks this truth against the false narrative that because of Pharaoh's earthly power structures he is a god worthy of worship. . . .
>
> If God is God, then Pharaoh is not. If God is God, then Caesar is not. If God is God, then the president of the

United States is not, the government is not, the military is not, and the legal system is not. He is God alone!

God told Moses to tell the people truth about the great I Am. The problem with Pharaoh and Egypt is they think they have more power than they actually do, and the problem with us is that too often we believe them.

Natasha Sistrunk Robinson, *A Sojourner's Truth*

Group Discussion

1. What are some of the ways that you prepare for spiritual battle?

2. We know that praise and worship provide opportunities to engage in spiritual battle. What are the battle songs that have been shared or passed on throughout generations? What are the battle songs that you will pass on to the next generation?

3. What is the most important lesson that you want to teach the next generation about God? What do you want them to always remember?

4. The Israelites now have one victory under their belt, but they have no idea what lies ahead for them. How do you prepare an uncertain people for what's new?

5. As a community, how will we spiritually and practically prepare the next generation for what's next?

Becoming New Leaders in a New Kingdom

---

*By the grace God has given me, I laid a foundation
as a wise builder, and someone else is building on it.
But each one should build with care. For no one can
lay any foundation other than the one already laid,
which is Jesus Christ. If anyone builds on this foundation
using gold, silver, costly stones, wood, hay or straw,
their work will be shown for what it is, because the
Day will bring it to light. It will be revealed with fire,
and the fire will test the quality of each person's work.*

1 Corinthians 3:10–13

Day 1

Commentary

SCRIPTURE READING
Exodus 18–19

SUPPLEMENTAL READING
Numbers 12

The book of Exodus is a bifid book, meaning that it is organized purpose-fully into two parts. The first part of the book is in narrative form, but between chapters 18 and 19, there is a shift to focus on God's instructions which shape Israel's new community. Much of the law codes are recorded in the books of Deuteronomy and Leviticus, though Exodus does include the core of the law—what we refer to as the Ten Commandments.[1]

Part of the challenge with reading this part of the text is the timeline. It is easy to assume that things are happening in chronological order, but it is questionable whether the events recorded in chapter 18 come after the Amalekites' defeat and before the presentation of the Ten Commandments recorded in chapter 19. Some scholars believe that the history of the ten plagues covered a period of approximately eighteen months. The point is: for modern-day and Western readers, we will do ourselves a great service if we slow down to process these events, while asking thoughtful questions

---

1   Translated to mean "ten words" in Hebrew and in the Greek Decalogue (*dekálogos*).

about what we observe or don't observe in the text. Before focusing on the Ten Commandments, let's consider what the narrative tells us about the people, how they interact with God and each other.

At the beginning of chapter 18, Moses's father-in-law, Jethro,[2] came to meet him in the desert after hearing all that God had done to deliver the Israelites from the hand of Pharaoh. Jethro is referred to as a priest, so my first question was, "What kind of priest was he?" The Bible doesn't tell us, but we know that he was not an Israelite, so we can safely assume that he was a pagan worshipper who served multiple deities. When he heard about what the God of the Israelites had done, he came to worship the Hebrew God as well. Moses welcomes Jethro with open arms and trusts his wise counsel.

Family Drama

The Bible records that Jethro brought Zipporah, his daughter and Moses's wife, and their two sons, Gershom and Eliezer, with him when he came to visit Moses in the desert. We know that Zipporah initially returned to Egypt with Moses (Exodus 4:18–26), but at some point Moses sent her away. When Moses returned to Egypt with Zipporah, their second son was not yet born. It is possible that he sent Zipporah away for her own safety, but we know that other women and children made the difficult journey out of Egypt. Their second son's name, Eliezer—meaning "My father's God was my helper; he saved me from the sword of Pharaoh" (18:4)—implies that he was born sometime after Moses's victory over Pharaoh.

The sons' ages are unknown at the time of this family reunion. Regardless, we do know that boys grow up to become men, but we do not hear much about either of them for the rest of Israel's recorded history. In a patriarchal society, it is normal for sons—especially the firstborn son—to learn and then take on the trades, roles, and responsibilities of their fathers.

---

2   Jethro is also called Hobab (Numbers 10:29) and Reuel (Exodus 2:18) in other Old Testament texts.

We see this happening with Jacob's sons, who became shepherds like their father, and Aaron's sons, who become priests like their father. However, Joshua stands in as a surrogate son to perform the duties that we normally would expect Moses's firstborn son to do. Something is awry either in the marriage, in the family, or with Zipporah's unwillingness to submit exclusively to the lordship of Yahweh.

The book of Numbers, chapter 12, only complicates the situation. There we find Moses's siblings, Miriam and Aaron, talking about him. Our Western eyes and curiosity are easily drawn to their questions, "Has the LORD spoken only through Moses? . . . Hasn't he also spoken through us?" (v. 2). Sibling rivalries are a thing. We know these people. We also know those who are jealous or covetous about the progress, position, and prosperity of others, when they have no real understanding of the sacrifices, commitments, or intentionality made by the leaders who hold the mantle. No doubt Miriam and Aaron are both leaders. We saw Miriam's leadership early when her parents entrusted her to watch over her brother as he floated in the Nile, and she advocated on his behalf when the princess drew him out of the water. We saw Aaron's leadership at work when God called him to become Moses's partner and speaker. Miriam became a prophetess (Exodus 15:20) and Aaron became a priest, but God only metaphorically spoke to Moses "face to face" (Numbers 12:8). God's relationship with Moses was intimate and special, but that was not their only issue. Slow. Down. Reader . . . or you will miss it. Before God talks about Moses, renders his judgment on Miriam, or chastises Aaron, we are told, "Miriam and Aaron began to talk against Moses because of his Cushite wife, for he had married a Cushite" (v. 1).

We are told twice in some translations of this verse that Moses's wife was a Cushite! There are differing views as to whether this wife is Zipporah, though we know that Zipporah was a Midianite. We also know that there are large chunks of time in Moses's life for which we have no record. We presume that Moses was a young man, perhaps forty years old

(Acts 7:23), when he fled Egypt. We know that he remained in Midian until the Pharaoh, the one who wanted to kill him, died. We know that he was eighty years old when he returned to Egypt (Exodus 7:7), but we don't know much about what happened between his original departure from Egypt and his arrival in Midian, his personal life in Midian, his marriage with Zipporah, or any other details after he returned to Egypt and was reunited with his family in chapter 18.

There are levels to this thing. Whether one or two wives, we know that Moses *did not* marry a Jewish woman. We may empathize that for a significant part of his young adult life, there were no Jewish women around to marry, but we must come to understand that his marriage(s) present a leadership issue and point of compromise, especially when he is going to call the Israelites to marry within the Jewish community.[3] The issue among the Israelites and intermarriage with other people groups was *not* about racial or ethnic concerns as we think of them today, but more about who or what the other people groups worshipped.[4]

God is holy, and He wants His people to become holy.[5] They will *not* be holy if they are married or yoked to people who are *not* solely devoted to Yahweh. It is possible that Miriam and Aaron had a concern for God's holiness when raising the issue about Moses's marriage. That's an unlikely motivation because God doesn't stand in agreement with them. We don't see God negatively address Moses's marriage situation. Perhaps Moses was heartbroken about the state of his marriage and that is why he sent Zipporah away, ignored, and maybe neglected her.[6] Maybe he considered

---

3   Reference Numbers 25 and Deuteronomy 7.

4   Reference Numbers 25, Deuteronomy 7, and the consequences of Israel's disobedience in this area can also be found in Ezra 10.

5   Leviticus 11:44–45; 19:2; 1 Peter 1:15–16.

6   Remember Zipporah's response when circumcising their firstborn son, Gershom, in Exodus 4:24–26. While some praise her for responding in obedience to God's covenantal command, others suggest that she did so grudgingly with the mysterious statement, "Surely you are a bridegroom of blood to me." If the latter is true, then Zipporah and her father may have taken different postures toward Moses's God. That would explain the casualness that Moses displays toward her in this chapter when contrasted to the openness Moses has toward her father, Jethro (Exodus 18:7–12 and Numbers 10:29–32). If Zipporah continued as a pagan worshipper, then Moses must rid himself of her. We see this type of separation again in Ezra 10.

his family a distraction and that is why we never hear from her or their sons again.

There is yet another layer to this. Cush was normally associated with Ethiopia, the southern region of Egypt, or northern Sudan (all countries geographically located in what we now refer to as the continent of Africa). Whether beautiful or undesirable we do not know, but we do know that Moses's Cushite wife was a Black woman. We read in Jeremiah 13:23, "Can an Ethiopian [or Cushite] change his skin or a leopard its spots? Neither can you do good who are accustomed to doing evil." The implication for the original hearers of this passage is: *In the same way that you can't change Black skin or remove a leopard's spots, you also can't turn those who are intent on doing evil into people who do good.*

It is not difficult to contrast the siblings speaking against the Black woman that Moses married with God's judgment of making Miriam leprous, turning her skin "white as snow" (Numbers 12:10). While racism isn't present in the text in the ways that we understand or articulate today, there is certainly an element of colorism at work in the passage. Colorism is when people show favoritism or partiality, prejudice or discrimination based on the complexion of one's skin, and this can happen among people within the same ethnic groups. Colorism means that we sometimes subconsciously determine who is "in" or "out" of our community based on their melanin levels. From Miriam and Aaron's perspective, they were "in," and the Cushite woman was "out." With His words and actions, God communicates to them in no uncertain terms that He determines who is "in"— God is riding with Moses, and the rest of them are along for that ride. Furthermore, God has the power at any moment to take them from a privileged position and put them outside of the "in" group. Watch out, Miriam![7]

---

7   Exegeting why Aaron did not suffer the same judgment as Miriam is beyond the scope of this study. However, I will share briefly what we can gather from other passages in the Torah. Being leprous would have made Aaron, the high priest, ceremonially unclean, and thus would have negatively impacted the entire community. Therefore, I submit that it is his title or role as high priest (not his gender, as some pastors presume) that causes God's grace to cover Aaron's sin and saves Aaron from God's judgment. We see God's gracious covering of Aaron again during the golden calf episode (Exodus 32:21–29). That communal sin

Families can be messy, and our personal relationships can directly impact the effectiveness and integrity of our leadership. Moses is the leader of God's choosing. Like so many of us, he is not a perfect human, but he is God's human—the agent that God chose for a particular time to bring about God's good will on the earth. Moses is the one who will guide the people in the ways of the Lord. He will need his family's support, and community leaders who are not jealous, covetous, or fighting inwardly, so they can all fulfill their respective roles when building a new kingdom of God's people.

As a Gentile, Jethro's presence at this point in the story presents valuable insights. When he heard about the faithfulness, power, and deliverance that the God of the Israelites offered, he said, "Praise be to the LORD, who rescued you from the hand of the Egyptians and of Pharaoh. . . . Now I know that the LORD is greater than all other gods, for he did this to those who treated Israel arrogantly" (Exodus 18:10–11). This pagan leader responded better than the Israelites whom God delivered! He affirmed his belief with a covenant by having a sacrificial meal with Aaron and the elders, and by making burnt offerings to the Lord. Like the circumcision of the non-Israelites within the community, Jethro is another example of God's grace extending to anyone who believes.

Questions

What hope does the text offer those who desire a relationship with God?

What relationship challenges do you see arise with increased responsibilities of leadership?

---

was so grievous that God was willing to destroy the entire community. As high priest, Aaron should have restrained the will of the people, but instead, he played a direct role in their idol worship. As a result, God killed three thousand people who were complicit in this blatant sin, but again, Aaron was not one of them. Additionally, we are told that no one can enter the Lord's presence or "see [His] face" and live (33:20); yet, God allows Aaron and his sons to enter his presence, and they all live (24:9–11). In this, God's word remains true, "I will have mercy on whom I will have mercy, and I will have compassion on whom I will have compassion" (Exodus 33:19).

Learning New Skills and Leadership Lessons

SCRIPTURE READING
Exodus 18:1–12

SUPPLEMENTAL READING
Acts 6:1–7; Matthew 25:14–30

After their covenantal meal, Jethro observed Moses operating in his role as community judge. Throughout the next day and into the evening, the people brought their issues to Moses and he made a determination of rightness between them. (For an example of this practice, read 1 Kings 3:16–28.) Upon observation, Jethro said, "What is this you are doing for the people? Why do you alone sit as judge, while all these people stand around you from morning till evening?" (Exodus 18:14). Unlike Miriam and Aaron in the previous lesson, Jethro was neither jealous nor questioning Moses's leadership ability. He observed Moses overworking himself while other people stood around idle, passive, and disengaged. He challenged Moses to put God's people to work.

Moses replied, "Because the people come to me to seek God's will. Whenever they have a dispute . . . I decide between the parties and inform them of God's decrees and instructions" (vv. 15–16). Moses was telling the truth. He was fulfilling this role because God spoke with him directly and told him the right things to do. The Israelites did not have that intimate relationship with the Lord. This is where Jethro offers his insight and mentorship. He replied, "What you are doing is not good. You and these people who come to you will only wear yourselves out. The work is too heavy for you; you cannot handle it alone." (vv. 17–18)

Jethro offers Moses wisdom, and it is imperative that we discern and take wisdom from people that we trust. Before returning to Egypt, Moses spent years in Midian observing Jethro among his family, within his work environment, and in his communal context. Moses held Jethro in such high regard that he persuaded Jethro to become a scout for Israel in the desert and to go with them into the promised land. Moses also promised to share whatever goods or blessings God provided with Jethro (Numbers 10:29–32). It appears that Jethro didn't take Moses up on that offer (Exodus 18:27), but it's safe to conclude that Moses knew and trusted Jethro. Every time we see these two men interact in the text, their relationship appears amicable. While Exodus 18:12 leads us to believe that Jethro pledged his allegiance to Yahweh and denounced all other deities, that doesn't mean that he got divine wisdom immediately. It's probable but not necessarily definitive. Jethro, like all humans, is an image bearer of God, and I am of the belief that all truth is God's truth. John Calvin expanded on this understanding when he wrote, "All truth is from God; and consequently, if wicked men have said anything that is true and just, we ought not to reject it; for it has come from God."[8] It is an act of humility for leaders to listen to wise counsel, discern God's will, and accept the mentorship of others.

It's early in the exodus journey. Moses needed to avoid burnout, and the people needed to make a change so they wouldn't get discouraged while

---

8   John Calvin, Alister McGrath & J.I. Packer, eds., *The Crossway Classic Commentaries, 1 and 2 Timothy and Titus*, Crossway Classic Commentaries, ed. Alister McGrath and J. I. Packer (Wheaton, IL: Crossway Books, 1998), 187.

waiting for Moses's judgments. In Jethro's instructions, we see practical leadership lessons and new skills to practice:

1. *Focus on your work.* Through my business, T3 Leadership Solutions, Inc., I provide coaching to high-caliber leadership executives. I find myself asking leaders the critical question, "What is uniquely yours to do?" As a coach, Jethro clarified Moses's unique responsibility when he said, "You must be the people's representative before God and bring their disputes to him" (Exodus 18:19). Nobody else in the community can do that. That alone is Moses's responsibility. We see the same clarity offered by the apostles in Acts 6:2–4, "It would not be right for us to neglect the ministry of the word of God in order to wait on tables. . . . [We] will give our attention to prayer and the ministry of the word." All God's work is important, and that's why it is critical for *all* God's people to accept their responsibility to engage in God's work. Waiting on tables is important because people need to eat to survive. Therefore, someone needs to accept that work responsibility. This leads us to understanding the second leadership skill:

2. *Share the responsibilities of leadership.* If a primary leadership question is, "What is uniquely mine to do?" then a secondary question of discernment can be, "What is right to do?" My friend Emily Freeman would ask, "What is your next right thing?" Another way of presenting the question given this context is, "How do we fill the leadership gaps?" We fill gaps by sharing the responsibilities of leadership, and we cannot share leadership responsibility with anybody! Jethro advises Moses to select the right leaders and then train them in the ways of God. "Teach them his decrees and instructions, and show them the way they are to live and how they are to behave. But select capable men from all the people—men who fear God, trustworthy men who hate dishonest gain—and appoint them as officials over thousands, hundreds, fifties and tens" (Exodus 18:20–21).

Moses has the responsibility for selecting leaders, and that's a new skill that he must develop. Selecting the right leaders is an accountability check with quality control measures which include:

- Questions of competence—Are the potential leaders capable; can they get the job done?
- Questions of faith—Do the potential leaders have a holy reverence for God? What evidence do you have of their conviction? In Acts 6:3, the apostles are encouraged to select leaders who have a reputation for being full of the Spirit and having wisdom.
- Questions of integrity—Are the potential leaders honest? Do they tell the truth? Do they follow through on their word? Can you trust them, and how do you know that they are trustworthy?
- Questions concerning the heart—Specifically, Jethro says that the potential leaders should "hate dishonest gain." This statement is about the condition of one's heart. We must discern: How does the potential leader understand their work responsibilities? Do they take shortcuts? What is their relationship with money? Are they greedy? What is their propensity to take a bribe? What reputation do they have in the community and in their workplace?

Even if the potential leaders meet basic requirements, even the spiritual ones, that does not necessarily mean that you should share responsibility with them. Although skilled, they may not be the right people for your ministry, business, network, or organization. My nonprofit organization, Leadership LINKS, Inc., has a creed and part of it reads, "God has strategically placed me in the RIGHT place, at the RIGHT time, and connected me to the RIGHT people to fulfill the purpose He has for my life." Sometimes you have the right people, but your place is not their place. Sometimes you have the right people and the right place, but the timing is off.

Equally important, Jethro said to "appoint them as officials over thousands, hundreds, fifties and tens." In the same way, Jesus presented a parable of the talents. (Take a moment to read Matthew 25:14–30 now.) The premise of Jethro's admonishment and Jesus's parable is: Everybody can't handle everything. Some people can only handle ten tasks or ten talents.

Some people will invest five talents and get five in return. Others have a ministry that will reach thousands. Some managers are excellent, but they will make poor C-suite executives. Some women and men can manage a household and a corporate office, and some cannot. There are great leaders in one field who are horrible in others. Men do not have a leadership gene; some men are terrible leaders; we can name them and the aftermath of their destruction. The point is, for those of us who have the responsibility of selecting leaders, we need to discern: Who? For what purpose? When and why now?

We are all at different stages of our leadership journey, but we must know that *all* Christians are called to leadership, and we must *all* be attentive to how we cultivate our leadership skills and prepare for God's kingdom work. One of the reasons that I love 1 Corinthians 12 is because it informs us of the visible evidence that the Holy Spirit is collectively at work among Christian people metaphorically as "the body of Christ." Regardless of our spiritual gifts, acts of services, or the type of work that we do, as Christians, we are *all* called to work—and that work is not divided into sacred or secular understandings and activities. This flawed perception is part of the reason so many Christians, especially women, marginalized people groups, and those without formal titles, are sitting on the sidelines waiting for a judgment or permission from others to confirm what God has already told them to do. There is a critical need for godly leadership, so we need to get to work!

> **Everybody can't handle everything.**

I appreciate the simple way that Elder Jason Williams defined work. He said, "Work is an effort that produces a result."[9] He also said, "Work is worship." Worship is not just for the Christian community. Worship is

---

9   Jason Williams, "Together (Part 7) | Jason Williams," King's Park International Church, June 7, 2021, https://www.youtube.com/watch?v=LJH4qZGyHD8&t=693s.

primarily about God, directing attention to Him, and affirming the grandeur of His name. This means that people outside of the faith community can experience our leadership and see the God of our work. God was clear when working to deliver the Israelites that He wanted them, the Egyptians, and all watching people groups to see and know that He alone is the Lord. This theological understanding, along with the statement "work is worship," gets to the heart of Matthew 5:16: "Your light must shine before people in such a way that they may see your good works, and glorify your Father [God] who is in heaven" (NASB).

We must be good workers regardless of our job, tasks, or level of responsibility! Being a leader over tens isn't a bad thing and being a leader over thousands isn't necessarily a good one. Being fearful of work, unwilling to invest or to accept the leadership responsibilities and tasks that God offers you, is slothfulness and it is sin (25:24–30). *Are you the right person, in the right place, and are you exercising your leadership at the right time and in the right way?* If we can select and train the right leaders who say "yes" to these discerning questions, then we will see the body of Christ positioned and functioning as God desires in the mutually beneficial, mutually submissive, and harmonious way that Paul writes about in 1 Corinthians 12.

Questions

What work has God called you to, and how do you exercise leadership in your work?

What new leadership skills do you need to learn for your current responsibilities?

What is your process for selecting new leaders?

Day 3

The Heavy Burden of Leadership

SCRIPTURE READING/REVIEW
Exodus 18:13–27

SCRIPTURE READING
1 Corinthians 12

Selecting and sharing leadership responsibilities with the right people at the right time is important. Moses also has the responsibility for training these leaders. How we approach training, both for the persons who are selecting leaders and those who are being considered for leadership, is critical. In this chapter, Moses is considering leaders to fulfill the role and take on the responsibilities of judge. Effective training helps us discern the roles where people are best suited. In leadership training, we are not simply determining what they can handle (that is a matter of their capacity and competence which we explored yesterday). We must also assess their availability. In this case, I'm not asking whether they have the time to commit to the thing that you are asking them to lead (that is a question to ask during the leadership selection process). In our Western culture, people will tell you that they are overcommitted or don't have time to commit to one more thing. As Christians and kingdom-minded leaders, however, we need to challenge each other to regularly evaluate how we prioritize the sacred time that God has given us *all* to invest in His kingdom.

During the training process, you get to test potential leaders' availability. Jethro said, "Let them judge the people at all times" (Exodus 18:22 ESV). Then the Bible records that the selected leaders "judged the people at all times." (v. 26 ESV). Training allows you to confirm people's willingness to serve others. If leaders are unwilling to commit to the process of training, then they are not going to consistently follow through on the heavy responsibilities of leadership. In training, you get to see how leaders prioritize, and whether they

> **People need selfless leaders who will serve them with integrity and an open heart.**

have prepared and planned well. You get to witness how they consistently show up and follow through. In training, you observe if they understand and accept the responsibility of leadership, have a teachable posture, a humility to learn, and an eagerness to share what they know, if they meet or exceed expectations, are effective communicators, how they respond to an offense, and how they work with others on the leadership team.

If two overarching leadership selection questions are *What is uniquely mine to do?* and *What is right to do?* then the first leadership training question can be: *Are the potential candidates available to serve others with a willingness to do the important work of leadership?* People need selfless leaders who will serve them with integrity and an open heart. Unfortunately, there are too many people who grab at the titles of leadership or influence for all the wrong reasons, mostly because leadership is about them. Then there are other potential leaders who model the behavior of the Israelites and respond like disobedient children.

I'm the oldest of three. My brother was an infant when he came into our home, and it was the first time that I experienced my parental instincts. I loved caring for him and watching him grow. I remember when he began speaking. We would ask him to do something, and he would respond, "I can't/don't wanna [insert whatever it is we asked him to do]." In the early stages of his development, it was difficult for him to distinguish between whether he could do something, and whether he wanted to do it. If we are honest, too many adult believers respond in this way when presented with the opportunity for leadership. Perhaps they tell themselves that they can't before they even try. They eliminate themselves because of fear, the lack of confidence, or some other reason. If we are honest, at other times, people simply don't want to rise to the challenge or accept the responsibility of leadership God has presented. Leadership is a heavy burden that should not be taken lightly. Contrary to popular belief, none of us have it all together when we are first called to leadership, and that's why we need to submit to the training process. Moses's adult life is a testimony to this truth. *Are you available to answer God's call to leadership? Will you respond in obedience when God invites you to work?*

Another leadership training question to consider is: *What is my position in this mission?* Knowing one's position can be different than understanding one's responsibility. On one hand, we all have a shared responsibility as a community of faithful believers, and as citizens of God's kingdom, but we do not all have the same roles. Paul wrote, "There are different kinds of gifts, but the same Spirit distributes them. There are different kinds of service, but the same Lord. There are different kinds of working, but in all of them and in everyone it is the same God at work" (1 Corinthians 12:4–6. Read verses 7 through 11).

Paul makes it clear that we do not all have the same leadership roles (vv. 28–30). Before mentioning them, he shared the importance of our being united in submission to the Holy Spirit, and the acceptance of our shared responsibility, while understanding each other's roles and working together to promote the common good of all humans (vv. 7, 15–20). We need each other on this faith and leadership journey (v. 21–27). While it is essential that we are connected to the right people, in the right place, at the right time, best-selling author Jim Collins says that it is vital that we also get the right people in the right seats.

Moses was selecting leaders who could fulfill the roles of judge, and because the judges didn't know God's ways, Moses had to train them so they could effectively settle disputes within the community in a manner that was honoring to God. We must not forget that these were formerly enslaved people, and the only way they know how to live is what they have witnessed and experienced in Egypt. Egypt is not the Lord's way! Therefore, Moses must teach and train these leaders, and give them increasing opportunities to practice. Jethro instructed Moses to have the new judges settle small disputes first, and then bring the difficult cases to Moses (Exodus 18:22). This is how Moses started to assign roles, set up leadership structures, and establish God-honoring systems within the new community that God was building among His people. Moses had to do this because of the heavy burden of leadership, and because Moses himself was fulfilling a unique leadership role as a builder.

Questions

How do you determine your leadership responsibilities?

What are the spiritual gifts and skills that you invest in to advance God's kingdom?

What leadership training can you offer in your church, workplace, or community?

Leading as a Builder

SCRIPTURE READING
1 Corinthians 3:10–13

Building and charting new territory is hard work. That's why Jethro told Moses to select, train, and assign leaders to their perspective roles. If Moses followed Jethro's advice, he would lighten his burden of leadership; building would be easier; he would get relief and avoid burnout; he would also have other leaders to share in the communal responsibilities (Exodus 18:22–23). If the other communal leaders accept and commit to their roles and responsibilities, then the builder can focus on his or her unique role.

Builders have the responsibility of creation, and they never create alone. They cast vision about what is possible and make people hopeful when pursuing God's ways, even when the way ahead looks bleak. Builders define and embody the values and ethos of a community. They create culture. Under God's direction, the judges in this passage will follow Moses's leadership when setting standards and boundaries for the health and wellness of the community. Builders must set clear direction by first defining *where* we are.

Moses to the people: *We just got out of Egypt. Pharaoh is no longer master over you. We will live for God in the promised land.*

Then builders must define *who* we are as a people, what we are doing, and where we are going together. Moses to the people: *God is your new master, and He is the only one that you will serve.*

Builders keep the vision, purpose, and mission in front of the people because building is hard work, and it is easy for people to get distracted or discouraged if they do not understand their "why" or see immediate results. When the road gets tough, and the journey is long, or the people have lost their way, it is good to know: *We are God's children, and He will not abandon us. We are not alone.* Builders must also inspire the community by reminding them of their identity, responsibilities, and the bigger kingdom mission—they are God's representatives or ambassadors to all the watching peoples on the earth.

Because of their unique role, it is tempting for builders to become prideful about the trust that God has placed in them or take advantage of the people that God has placed in their care. That is why builders need to humbly submit to the leadership, wise counsel, and mentorship of others. Moses models this humility in his relationship with Jethro, but he does not follow Jethro blindly. Moses listened carefully to Jethro's counsel (Exodus 18:24). He considered if it was the way of God (v. 23). Then he tested or implemented the advice (vv. 25–26). This is the unique challenge of building. Builders must be willing to take risks, test out or try new ideas to see if they work. If they don't, it's not necessarily sin and it's not the end of the world. Keep your family, your community, your church, or organization focused on the ultimate leader who is God, and the vision and values that He has provided for all of you to share the responsibilities of leadership in the new initiative that you are undertaking together, even when you fail.

Reflection Exercise

What are your current leadership roles and responsibilities either professionally or personally? In what areas do you need help? What leadership training, mentorship, coaching, or support might you need to follow through on to complete the work that God has assigned to you? Schedule a meeting with a mentor to discuss this personal assessment.

Becoming a Priesthood and a Holy Nation

SCRIPTURE READING
Exodus 19

SUPPLEMENTAL READING
1 Peter 2:4–12; Revelation 5:9–10

Three months into their exodus journey, the Israelites find themselves at Mount Sinai, the same mountain where God said to Moses, "I will be with you. And this will be the sign to you that it is I who have sent you: *When you have brought the people out of Egypt, you will worship God on this mountain*" (Exodus 3:12, emphasis added). Let's honor God for fulfilling this promise to Moses. As the people set up camp, Moses went up the mountain to speak to God. God provided this casuistic law (or conditional instruction) for the descendants of Jacob: "*If* you obey me fully and keep my covenant, *then* out of all nations you will be my treasured possession. Although the whole earth is mine, you will be for me a kingdom of priests and a holy nation" (19:5–6, emphasis added). The call to leadership in God's new kingdom is not just for priests and judges; the call to leadership is for the entire community. When Moses went down the mountain to tell the community about their great leadership responsibility, the people replied together, "We will do everything the LORD has said" (v. 8).

Building a New Kingdom

You can read Jesus's teaching about the kingdom of God or the kingdom of heaven in several parables.[10] Although people across the world have become fascinated with Britain's longest reigning monarch, Queen Elizabeth II, the celebrity and adornment of Princess Diana before her untimely demise, and the royal exodus of Prince Harry and Meghan Markle, most people in the modern world have not experienced and therefore do not understand what it means to live under a monarchy, certainly not an oppressive one like the Israelites experienced in Egypt. We must not forget that the Israelites lived in a kingdom, and if the Old Testament teaching is to inform our understanding of the New Testament, then we must have a basic knowledge of how kingdoms work, and why God calls His people to provide accountability for the leaders of the earthly kingdoms in this world, and bear alliance to His divine kingdom where His chosen people are set apart as His leaders and ambassadors oftentimes within flawed, broken, and spiritually bankrupt earthly kingdoms.[11]

There are four basic elements that define a kingdom:

1. Kingdoms are ruled by a king or queen who sets the standards of governance.
2. The ruler has subjects, people who submit to their leadership willingly or not.

---

10 Reference Luke 13:18–21 (also 17:20–21) and Matthew 13:1–52.
11 I am not saying in this sentence that we are not called to submit to the leadership or authority of civil or government leaders. I believe that we are (Romans 13:1–7; 1 Peter 2:13–15), specifically when they are fulfilling the leadership responsibility of creating a just society and are working for the common good of the people they are serving, and not their own self-interest (Matthew 20:25–28). I am saying, however, that as Christians, our chief authority and allegiance is to God, and we must, therefore, submit to His leadership above all else. It is dangerous when we confuse nationalism or xenophobia with our religious or faith convictions without seriously considering our Christian calling to leadership within earthly kingdoms (nations, governments, etc.) and among a people and earthly leaders who do not submit to God.

3. Kingdom rulers have royal heirs, who assume both the responsibility and the benefits of leading the kingdom at the opportune time.

4. Kingdoms have designated territories or land. Queen Elizabeth II is not the queen of everybody, everywhere. She is only a queen with authority in the United Kingdom and fifteen Commonwealth countries. She cannot go to the United States, or North Korea, or Israel, and start commanding their citizens with an expectation that we are going to submit to her leadership.

There are two ways to gain kingdom authority:

1. You are born an heir to the throne; normally this is the first-born child of the kingdom ruler. Queen Elizabeth II's firstborn, Charles, the Prince of Wales—not his siblings, Princess Anne, Prince Andrew, or Prince Edward, who are also heirs—is next in line for the throne.

2. You fight for the kingdom. The primary way that kingdoms switch hands is through the violence of war. We read about this throughout the Old Testament. Jesus is the only king who took territory in a nonviolent way, and that's an oxymoron because the earthly acknowledgment of His lordship required the violent sacrifice of His own life.

God is not like earthly kings! God's kingdom is unlimited, without land or territorial restrictions. It is a spiritual and physical kingdom, manifesting in heaven (or the spiritual realm), and on earth (the physical realm). God sets His own standards for His kingdom, over and apart from the standards of the earthly kingdoms in the world. God chooses His own heirs, and unlike earthly kingdoms, we can have multiple heirs all active and mobilized for work and leadership at the same time, while all receiving the gift of the Holy Spirit, and the benefits and blessings of God (Romans 8:1–17). There are no limitations with God! This foundation gives us a practical understanding of what God is doing among the Israelites and through His New Testament church.

By making a covenant with Israel, God is establishing himself as a powerful king or suzerain[12] to Israel, the vassal (or weaker nation) that is switching their allegiance from Pharaoh's kingdom. The Mosaic covenant follows an Ancient Near Eastern covenant structure of preamble, prologue, stipulations, sanctions, witnesses, and documentation.[13] The preamble identifies the person making the covenant. God is making the covenant with Israel. The prologue defines the relationship between the covenanting parties. In this chapter (Exodus 19:4) and throughout the Exodus narrative, God names himself as the one who brought Israel out from under Egypt's enslavement (20:2). The stipulations are the laws of the contractual relationship. In this case, it is the "Sinai covenant" or "Mosaic covenant" presented in Exodus 19–24. The sanctions are the blessings that are outlined and presented for their obedience, and the curses or judgments that will come to the community because of their disobedience. We see different patterns of witnesses in the Torah,[14] but we must know that God is an authoritative witness unto himself (Isaiah 45:23; Hebrews 6:13, 17)! And the final part of the covenant structure is documentation, which is the Ten Commandments crafted on stone.

Building a Priesthood

God has already set His affection upon the Israelites, calling them His "treasured possession." He has shown them mercy despite their sin and rebellion, and He has saved them from the grips of Pharaoh and

---

12 *Yahweh* alone is the King of Kings and Lord of Lords.
13 From Old Testament summary notes from Dr. Douglas Stuart, professor of Old Testament, Gordon-Conwell Theological Seminary.
14 See examples of this in Deuteronomy 4:26 and 30:19.

Egypt. Their salvation was physical and spiritual so that Israel could see, know, and experience God's essence and intention toward them. So, the presentation of the law is not about the Israelites working to gain God's favor; they already have it! The law teaches them how to respond in the world as people who identify with a holy God as their sovereign. As "holy" people, they must reflect the will of their sovereign by sanctifying themselves for God's good purposes. "I am the LORD your God; consecrate yourselves and be holy, because I am holy" (Leviticus 11:44). They are to become a holy nation among unholy nations. "Moses conceives of Israel as living out its national life on the world's stage, and the obedience (or lack thereof) of the Israelites will prompt questions and admiration on the part of the nations. . . . One of the most important functions of the law, then, was to allow the Israelites to live a life that was different from the people around them."[15] This is the way they will fulfill God's promise to Abram and become a blessing to all nations (Genesis 12:2–3).

Being an American means that we value each other's individual rights, and this type of thinking is antithetical to the collective community that God seeks to build, whether the people of Israel or His New Testament church. The Bible is a Middle Eastern book that focuses on the collective or corporate body, and rarely the individual. We are to "live as free people, but . . . not use [our] freedom as a cover-up for evil; [but rather] live as God's slaves" (1 Peter 2:16). The new covenant reaffirms the truth of the old covenant: we are *free in* Christ, *and* we are *owned by* Christ. The law defines what uniquely sets Israel apart as God's people. It is the standard that characterizes their community, sustains and grows families, helps them navigate relationships, provides accountability for leadership, and distinguishes their tribes from the other peoples of the earth. God then called this new, holy nation to become a priesthood.

---

15   Peter T. Vogt, *Interpreting the Pentateuch: An Exegetical Handbook* (Grand Rapids, MI: Kregel Academic & Professional, 2009), 29.

We will learn that God has assigned the leadership role of priests to the tribe of Levi, and specifically to Aaron's descendants. Aaron and his sons were to become mediators between God and the people; however, God also says that Israel's entire nation is to become a kingdom of priests for Him. "Since Israel as a whole was envisioned as being a 'kingdom of priests,' the people for whom it would act as mediator were the Gentiles (non-Israelites). In other words, Israel was to serve as mediator for the rest of humanity."[16] This bears significance, not just for understanding the book of Exodus and the law, but also for understanding our leadership responsibilities as New Testament believers. Too often, Christian leaders focus on the priesthood of Aaron, but have not understood or been taught the significance of the priesthood of all believers. Quite frankly, some leaders like being the go-to person, the bottleneck, the person on whom everyone must depend or wait for answers so they can abuse their power and lord their leadership over others. Some leaders like uneducated, misinformed, and passive followers they can easily manipulate, but that is not God's desire for His people.

By the end of this study, we will come to understand the apostle Peter's desire for the New Testament church—not just local congregations but *all* Christians who are leading, working, and serving anywhere—to become a priesthood that represents Jesus to the rest of the world. Read what he wrote in 1 Peter 2:9–12.

Peter's instruction to God's chosen people echoes the words that God relayed to Moses: *As God's chosen people, you are already in intimate relationship with God; now reveal yourself to the world as a holy nation and royal priesthood; lead and represent me well so that when people see you, your actions, and your good works, they will glorify God.*

God is holy and cannot be associated with sin, so to preserve their lives until they learn His ways, God set up boundaries of protection for

---

16   Vogt, *Interpreting the Pentateuch*, 29.

them (Exodus 19:12–13, 21–24). He spoke directly to Moses through a cloud (vv. 9, 16) and fire (v. 18), while calling the people to consecrate themselves, prepare for proper worship, and receive His covenantal law.

Question

How does this teaching on kingdom and priesthood shape your theology and inform your relationship with God?

Building for a New Kingdom

Moses is exercising his leadership at the start of a new journey with Israel. It is a steep learning curve for all of them, so Moses enters God's presence to learn God's ways. God is going to build a holy nation and a people through the Israelites, and God is still building among His people today. That movement is happening in churches, nonprofits, advocacy groups, or charity organizations. It is also happening in boardrooms and courtrooms, laboratories and academic institutions, congressional halls and art centers, on sports fields and food trucks. God's kingdom has expanded everywhere, and that's exactly where His people need to work, lead, and build. We need spiritual guidance, practical tools, and the right relationships to build a strong and sustainable foundation wherever God has called us to work.

Offering mentorship and sponsorship are two ways we can exercise our redemptive influence to cultivate learning communities that facilitate the shared values of kingdom citizenship. Moses teaches us that building with a God-sized mission and influence takes a team approach. . . .

We need people in every generation who will educate, guide, and navigate for others. Those are some of the responsibilities of mentors. A mentor cultivates a relationship; they learn you and your story well and offer perspective for how that story fits within the context of God's great redemption story. And they are willing to journey with you on the road.

Sponsors, on the other hand, are the people who open doors and create opportunities to get you where God wants you to contribute. They are further along on their journey, so they get invitations and access to events, programs, networks, and opportunities when people on your level are not invited. Yet when sponsors go into those select rooms and enter into new networking relationships, they take your name and your story with them. They are setting you up for good! When building for a new kingdom, we need both mentors and sponsors.

Natasha Sistrunk Robinson, *A Sojourner's Truth*

Group Discussion

1. Time of sharing from this lesson's reflection exercise: What did you learn about yourself from your leadership assessment? How and when will you seek the support, spiritual direction, mentorship, or coaching needed to address your present leadership challenges?

2. God called Israel to become a holy nation. He calls the New Testament church to become a community. How does this teaching shape your

understanding of the New Testament church's responsibility to collectively become a community of believers who represent God on earth?

3. Who are you currently mentoring and who is mentoring you?

4. If you are a working professional, what opportunities do you have to sponsor others in your workplace, specifically those who are from marginalized people groups? Write down the names of at least three people you will intentionally begin sponsoring. Or ask yourself: Who in your field knows what sponsorship looks like and may be available for you to ask this important question?

5. What opportunities is God currently providing for us (individually and collectively) to work and advance His kingdom?

_____

_____

_____

_____

_____

_____

_____

_____

_____

_____

_____

_____

_____

_____

_____

_____

_____

_____

Introducing the Ten Commandments

*Do not think that I have come to abolish the Law
or the Prophets; I have not come to abolish them
but to fulfill them. . . . Therefore anyone who sets aside
one of the least of these commands and teaches others
accordingly will be called least in the kingdom of heaven,
but whoever practices and teaches these commands
will be called great in the kingdom of heaven.*

Jesus (Matthew 5:17, 19)

Commentary

SCRIPTURE READING

Exodus 20

SUPPLEMENTARY READING

Leviticus 19:1–18

When an expert in the law asked Jesus, "Which is the greatest command-ment?" Jesus replied, "'Love the Lord your God with all your heart and with all your soul and with all your mind.' This is the first and greatest commandment. And the second is like it: 'Love your neighbor as your-self.' All the Law and the Prophets hang on these two commandments" (Matthew 22:36–40).[1] Jesus began by quoting Deuteronomy 6:5 which says in effect, "Love the Lord with your entire being." Then, he quoted an excerpt from Leviticus 19:18, "Do not seek revenge or bear a grudge against anyone among your people, but love your neighbor as yourself. I am the LORD." God is the motivation for the Israelites' love of neighbor, and the command implies that they already love themselves. The Golden Rule in Matthew 7:12 presents the ethics of the greatest commandment: "So in everything, do to others what you would have them do to you, for

---

1   Also see Mark 12:28–33 and Luke 10:25–28.

this sums up the Law and the Prophets." Jesus is capturing the *spirit* of the law as the Israelites and prophets understood it.

The greatest commandment begins with the truth: we love God because God first loved us (1 John 4:19). John wrote, "Dear friends, since God so loved us, we also ought to love one another. No one has ever seen God; but if we love one another, God lives in us and his love is made complete in us" (vv. 11–12). Our choice to love others is motivated by God's choice to love us. Choosing to love others is evidence that the Holy Spirit is at work in us, making us a healthy, whole, and holy community. John continues to affirm the greatest commandment, "Whoever claims to love God yet hates a brother or sister is a liar. For whoever does not love their brother and sister, whom they have seen, cannot love God, whom they have not seen. And [God] has given us this command: Anyone who loves God must also love their brother and sister" (vv. 20–21). There is no way to cover the depth of the Ten Commandments given the scope of this study, but we must understand God's objective in the Decalogue as communicated to the Israelites, from Jesus's own lips, and from His disciples' teaching, is *to love God with our entire being and to love our neighbors as we love ourselves.*

> **God's objective in the Decalogue as communicated to the Israelites, from Jesus's own lips, and from His disciples' teaching, is *to love God with our entire being and to love our neighbors as we love ourselves.***

Introduction to the Decalogue

Why study the Ten Commandments? Read the psalmist's reasoning in Psalm 19:7–11. The psalmist doesn't feel oppressed by submitting to

God's law. Instead, he presents the benefits for heeding God's instructions: God's law brings refreshment to our souls, makes us wise, brings joy to our hearts, grants clear vision, affirms God's righteousness, warns us, and provides blessings and great rewards. Klaus Bockmuehl wrote that there are three applications for the Decalogue:

1. *Civil use.* The commandments are incorporated into the law of the land. They work to constrain evil, to hold back the potential criminal;

2. *Accusing use.* The theological technical term is *Usus elenchthicus*, meaning "reprimand, rebuke, accuse, condemn." The second use of the Law, then, is to convict the sinner of their sin (cf. Rom. 3:20); . . .

3. *Teaching use.* The Ten Commandments, shorn of their curse and condemnation, return to the regenerate believer as ethical instruction, lights by which to steer the life of sanctification.[2]

There are spiritual, communal, practical, ethical, and civil purposes for the law, and by heeding them, the Israelites will denounce their former ways of worship and civil allegiance, while collectively growing in maturity concerning God's teaching so their children can do the same (Romans 2). Therefore, we see positive and negative connotations for the law, yielding blessings for obedience and judgment for disobedience (Deuteronomy 28).

---

2   Klaus Bockmuehl, *The Christian Way of Living: An Ethics of the Ten Commandments* (Vancouver, British Columbia: Regent College Publishing, 1994), 22.

Questions

What was your impression of the Ten Commandments when you heard or read them for the first time?

How does your understanding of the greatest commandment relate to your understanding about the Ten Commandments?

Day 2

Knowing and Loving God

SCRIPTURE READING
Exodus 20:1–7

SUPPLEMENTAL READING
1 John 4; Deuteronomy 4:1–40; 5:1–11; 6; 11; 13

In this section, we will survey the first part of the Decalogue which focuses on Israel's relationship with God. I encourage you to complete the supplemental reading which provides more depth for the teachings. When training others concerning the greatest commandment, I reinforce the importance of knowing and loving God. The apostle John's school of theology spells love with a four-letter word . . . *obey*. "This is how we know that we love the children of God: by loving God and carrying out his commands. In fact, this is love for God: to keep his commands. And his commands are not burdensome" (1 John 5:2–3). John repeatedly records Jesus saying, "If you love me, keep my commands" (John 14:15); "Whoever has my commands and keeps them is the one who loves me" (v. 21); "Anyone who loves me will obey my teaching" (v. 23); "Anyone who does not love me will not obey my teaching" (v. 24).

I paused the first time I read a couple of sentences from Klaus Bockmuehl's book *The Christian Way of Living: An Ethics of the Ten Commandments*. He wrote, "How far do we let God determine our life? Perhaps our obedience is weak because our love is weak."[3] Ouch! The question was piercing, and the answer was painstakingly true. He continued, "Perhaps we care too much for the things of this world. Perhaps we live in a state of forgetfulness toward God. The first commandment reminds us of our true destiny, the thing for which we were created and redeemed: to love God, to listen to him, and to be obedient to his word."[4]

The first commandment is: "You shall have no other gods before me" (Exodus 20:3). Put simply: worship God and nothing or no one else. Judaism and Christianity are monotheistic faiths, meaning we worship one God. However, the Israelites lived in a polytheist society where people called on different gods for many purposes. There were gods who supposedly caused fertility, sent rain, caused crops to flourish, and reigned over certain territories. So, flourishing in their culture meant worshipping and sacrificing to different gods all the time. God is putting a full stop to this madness by calling the Israelites to worship him alone. "The first commandment is always a call to repentance because we are rarely single-minded in our commitment to God. The commandment, taken seriously, produces the response: God be merciful to me, a sinner [Luke 18:13]."[5]

We repent only when God acts first on our behalf (Romans 2:4). Remember, God chose to love, set His affections upon, and deliver the Israelites. Now, He is calling them to respond to the intimate relationship being offered. To live freely in God, they must reject and turn their affections away from other false gods. Because God's grace is already at work, we can see early in the Bible how God's loving-kindness leads His people to repentance.

---

3   Klaus Bockmuehl, *The Christian Way of Living: An Ethics of the Ten Commandments* (Vancouver, British Columbia: Regent College Publishing, 1994), 48.

4   Bockmuehl, *The Christian Way of Living*, 48.

5   Bockmuehl, 33.

The second commandment is: "You shall not make for yourself an image in the form of anything in heaven above or on the earth beneath or in the waters below. You shall not bow down to them or worship them; for I, the LORD your God, am a jealous God" (Exodus 20:4–5). The false gods worshipped in Egypt were made of human hands. God repeatedly told Israel not to worship idols because they are impotent and can't do anything for the people (Psalm 115:1–13). In contrast, God reminded Israel of the miracles He accomplished on their behalf.

It is easy to point fingers at the Israelites for worshipping idols, while ignoring the idols we set up in our own hearts. People worship idols because they believe that they need them. You know that something has become an idol in your life when it is the first thing you think about when you rise or the last thing that you ponder before bed. An idol might be your phone or long work list, coffee or alcohol. There are all kinds of idols or "acceptable" sins that we allow in our lives which conflict with this commandment.

We cannot love God's ways and embrace the sinful ways of the world at the same time (1 John 2:15–17; 3:1–10; 4:1–6). We cannot love God and love money. We need money to live, but we cannot compromise God's standards to get it or keep it. Money may make our lives more comfortable, but it cannot save us from ourselves (Matthew 6:19–24). Money can be an enslaving master. Our economic culture of social media, celebrity worship, and overnight millionaire "influencers" can make us forget that we are also prone to idolize the praise and acceptance of others (John 12:41–43; Galatians 1:10; Acts 5:29).[6]

God says that He is jealous, but not in the same way that we are. God is essentially saying that He will not share His glory with anyone or anything else because none other is worthy of it. God is our sovereign, and

---

6 This temptation is perhaps more dangerous than we like to admit because we all want to be liked by others, and sometimes that causes us to compromise. However, we must not forget that the desire to please the crowd is one of the reasons that our Savior, Jesus, was passed through a kangaroo court to receive corporate punishment which resulted in the death penalty.

if we metaphorically "force His hand" to do something that is outside of His nature—that is, have the holy God share His glory or majesty with an unholy thing—there will be negative consequences. For this, God says that He will punish "the children for the sin of the parents to the third and fourth generation of those who hate me, but showing love to a thousand generations for those who love me and keep my commandments" (Exodus 20:5–6).

The Leader of Generations

God is the God of generations who regularly refers to himself as "the God of Abraham, Isaac, and Jacob." In Exodus 20:5–6, God is not saying that He will punish children for what their parents do, for each of us must give an account for our own actions before God (Romans 14:12). However, there is a cosmic reality that children are directly influenced by their parents' actions. If I die without any money in the bank or a life insurance policy, then my daughter must pay for my funeral and any remaining debt owed. When there is an addiction like alcoholism or a practice of domestic violence in the home, apart from God's grace, it is more likely that the children raised in those homes will become addicts, abusers, or victims themselves. Some call these traumatic experiences "generational curses." It is simply the biblical principle of blessing and cursing (read Deuteronomy 28), sowing and reaping. If you plant seeds of death, destruction, and hate, that is what you will harvest.

The negative implications of parents' actions *can* impact the third or fourth generations, but the blessings and promises for obedience linger for thousands of generations to those who love God and keep His commandments. This is why God tells the generations to create ways for communal remembrance and to reaffirm their commitment to the Lord.[7] So the grandmother's prayers reach way down the family line, as does

---

7   Deuteronomy 4:9–10, 23, 31; 6:1–2, 6–9; and 11:18–21.

the uncle's philanthropy, the aunt's activism, the cousin's kindness, the mother's truth-telling, the father's presence, and the grandfather's teaching. We can all bless our families, those present and not yet born, if we follow the Lord's way.

The third commandment says, "You shall not misuse the name of the LORD your God, for the LORD will not hold anyone guiltless who misuses his name" (Exodus 20:7). I wouldn't purchase an elegant evening gown to wear to a cookout, or don pearls to participate in a mud fight. Likewise, we should not take God's name—something that is precious—and use it in a way that is common. "A good translation of the commandment would be, 'You shall not use God's name in vain, inappropriately, improperly, trivially, idly, in an empty manner.'"[8] We must not use God's name in vain: "Oh my God!" We must not use God's name to make a vow, especially when we're not telling the truth. "I swear before God . . ." We certainly don't want to curse God's name. "Godd**n!" God's name is holy, and must be revered among God's people. God will find anyone guilty who blasphemes His name. On the contrary, there are proper ways to invoke the name of God, for God's name is always worthy of praise! "Let everything that has breath praise the LORD" (Psalm 150:6).

Question

What are some actions you can intentionally take to bless the next generation?

---

8   Bockmuehl, *The Christian Way of Living*, 60.

Day 3

God Loves Us

SCRIPTURE READING
Exodus 20:8–11; 31:12–17

SUPPLEMENTAL READING
Luke 10:25–37

God is love (1 John 4:8) and therefore God's people are to reflect love. The rest of the Decalogue focuses on how this love is shown through the "civil laws," a guide for Israel's love and respect for each other.[9] In the United States, there is chatter, particularly within the younger generations, about the negativity of our Christian cultural influence. They have a desire for being known "for" instead of "against" anything. This sounds like a good aspiration, but presents a theological problem. When giving instructions for much of the Decalogue, God uses negative language to express His holy standard against the acceptable standards of the culture to which the Israelites are accustomed. God's people must be sanctified in thought and action *from* the values and behaviors of people in society who do not have an intimate relationship with God. God says: *Do not* murder. *Do not* commit adultery. *Do not* steal. *Do not* give false testimony. *Do not* covet . . . In presenting the negative connotations, God is telling Israel what He loves

---

9   Consider Jesus's teaching in John 15:9–13, 17, which motivated Paul (Philippians 2:4–18).

and what He is for. *Do not murder.* God is *for* the preservation of life. *Do not commit adultery.* God is *for* protecting the sanctity of marriage. *Do not give false testimony.* God is *for* truth-telling. Therefore, God is using the Decalogue to communicate *and* train Israel to live as representatives *for* God, as they show love *for* their neighbor.

God Loves Rest

"Remember the Sabbath day by keeping it holy" (Exodus 20:8). We know that God gave the Israelites opportunities to practice the Sabbath before he outlined the formal commandment to keep it. God offered the Sabbath as a gift to the community. The Sabbath day is significant because (1) it is holy unto the Lord, (2) it provides the community an opportunity to rest and honor the Lord as their provider, and (3) it is a sign and celebration for generations about this covenant God is making with Moses. (Read Exodus 31:12–17.) God, who does not tire, modeled this rhythm of work and rest in creation for His people. If we don't rest, then work, accomplishment, and production can become idols—the things that we sometimes allow to define our identity. "Time and again our work crowds out our time for refreshment. But taking a break challenges the heart that craves ambition."[10] Keeping the Sabbath guards us from the deception that we don't need God because we can provide for ourselves.

The Sabbath is a gift to all of God's people. We don't keep the Sabbath because we must; that's legalism, and that's what Jesus spoke against in Mark 2:23–27.[11] We keep the Sabbath because we can, and with this invitation, God speaks to His beloved: *I love you. Rest awhile. I love you. You are more than what you produce. I love you. Enjoy the fruit of your labor. I love you. Spend time with your family and friends,*

---

10 Klaus Bockmuehl, *The Christian Way of Living: An Ethics of the Ten Commandments* (Vancouver, British Columbia: Regent College Publishing, 1994), 73.

11 Reference Luke 6:1–11; Matthew 12:1–7, 9–13; and John 5:1–9.

and play with the children in your community. I love you. Go check on your neighbor. I love you. Come away to get present with me and find rest for your weary soul.

Reflective Exercise

Take time this week to reflect on the past year of your life. Document the moments where you remember intentionally loving your neighbor or resting well. Over the course of the year, how did your relationships reflect your love of God, neighbor, and self? What days, seasons, or times did you feel the most alive? Be specific. Where were you when these sacred moments took place? How did you get there? What motivated you? Who was with you? Where was God in this sacredness? How was He speaking? It is often said, "If we fail to plan, we plan to fail." Look ahead either to the next month, quarter, or year. What is God's invitation in your preparation? Who will you invite on this sacred journey of perhaps establishing new sacred rhythms? Everything is better with a community.

God Loves
Human Relationships

SCRIPTURE READING
Exodus 20:12–14

SUPPLEMENTAL READING
Deuteronomy 5:16–18

God created humans in His own image or likeness to exercise dominion or leadership of all His good creation (Genesis 1:27–31). All humans have purpose, are created for leadership, and have a responsibility to reflect God's goodness on the earth. That divine stewardship begins with our relationship with God and continues through the healthy relationships that we cultivate with other humans. It is God, not humans, who determines how loving and healthy relationships are established and sustained in the world He created.

God Loves and Honors
the Role of Parents

The fifth command is: "Honor your father and your mother, so that you may live long in the land the LORD your God is giving you" (Exodus

20:12).[12] This is a commandment with promise (Ephesians 6:1–3), leading to a long life in the promised land. "The Hebrew root [for honor] is KBD, דּוֹבָכ . . . [which] means 'to make heavy.' So to honor is to take parents seriously, to place them high in one's order of priorities."[13] In the Israelites' "shame and honor" culture, love, honor, and respect were intertwined. Honor is uniquely practiced in diverse cultures. Parents and children may have different expectations of what "honoring" looks like within the context of their family, especially as children grow into adulthood. To avoid offense, families can communicate their expectations and love by seeking to meet each other's needs. This commandment specifically speaks against children striking or cursing their parents.[14]

Parenting can be a daunting task. It is a lifelong commitment, and a sacrificial act of love. The Bible has responsibilities for both parents and children in this regard. Children are to obey their parents, assuming that their parents are not leading them against the Lord's way (Colossians 3:20). Parents are not to provoke their children to anger, while bringing them up under the discipline and instruction of the Lord (Ephesians 6:4 and Colossians 3:21). There are countless ways that parents and children sin against and manipulate each other. With this command, God is calling children to love their parents. In the same way that our obedience to God reveals our love for Him, children's obedience reveals love for their parents and God. "The parents who reject the first commandment can expect their children to reject the fifth one. The parents who do not submit to God should not expect their children to submit to them."[15]

God Loves Human Life

The sixth commandment, "You shall not murder" (Exodus 20:13; Deuteronomy 5:17), speaks to the value of human life. God protects human

---

12   Reference Deuteronomy 5:16; 27:16.
13   Klaus Bockmuehl, *The Christian Way of Living: An Ethics of the Ten Commandments* (Vancouver, British Columbia: Regent College Publishing, 1994), 80.
14   Reference Exodus 21:17; Leviticus 20:9; Proverbs 20:20; Matthew 15:4; and Mark 7:10.
15   Bockmuehl, *The Christian Way of Living*, 85.

life and wants the Israelites to have a pro-life ethic. It is important to understand that the Bible makes a distinction between killing and murder. This commandment speaks against murder, specifically what we would refer to as manslaughter or premeditated murder. It speaks against murder that is born out of malice or deceit (Deuteronomy 27:24) and against murder of an innocent person (v. 25).

As a military veteran, I know that war is a tumultuous topic, and there is never a completely just party on either side of a bloody battle. Yet, in our fallen world where evil abounds, there are times for war and times for peace, times for life and times for death (Ecclesiastes 3:2, 8). There are many places in the Bible where God authorizes or allows the killing of human life, and we have seen that already in the Israelites' battle with the Amalekites. The Israelites will go to war to possess the promised land (Deuteronomy 20), and people will die. David asked God on numerous occasions whether he should pursue an enemy, and God gave His approval knowing that it would result in the loss of human life.

According to the law, the penalty for murder is always death. However, sometimes people are killed accidently. Someone could make a medical mistake or hit a jogger with their car at night when the jogger is wearing black on an unlit street. The law allows protection until the community can make a righteous judgment concerning the offender's actions that accidentally result in murder (Exodus 21:12–13). That's why God established the cities of refuge (Numbers 35:6–28; Deuteronomy 4:41–43; 19:1–13).

Murder is really about the condition of one's heart or one's attitude toward one's neighbor. Jesus spoke to this heart issue and unconstrained anger in Matthew 5:21–24. The Torah calls into question malicious intent concerning one's neighbor, and whether anger drove the killer to take his neighbor's life. If the answer is yes as confirmed by at least two witnesses, then the offender is guilty of murder, and the community must put the killer to death.

God Loves the Marriage Covenant

The commandment "You shall not commit adultery" (Exodus 20:14; Deuteronomy 5:18) reveals God's love and protection of marriage.[16] Leviticus 20:10 expounds upon this matter: "If a man commits adultery with another man's wife—with the wife of his neighbor—both the adulterer and the adulteress are to be put to death."[17] This community standard carried over into the New Testament, which is why it was risky for Jesus's mother to say yes to God as an engaged woman. When her pregnancy was revealed, it was assumed that she committed adultery, the penalty of which was death.

The spirit of the law is to love your spouse as your neighbor and not to offend him or her by committing adultery. The call is also to love your neighbor enough so as not to touch his or her spouse in a sexual way, which connects to the commandment about coveting anything within your neighbor's territory. When Jesus spoke about this commandment, he raised the standard again to address heart issues (Matthew 5:27–32). "You have heard that it was said, 'You shall not commit adultery.' But I tell you that anyone who looks at a woman lustfully has already committed adultery with her in his heart" (vv. 27–28).

We live in a culture where sex is used to sell nearly everything. I've been to more than enough women's ministry events that teach about modesty and purity, which are holy standards. However, I believe we can invite more conversations among women and men about the honoring of our own bodies as holy unto the Lord, and the self-discipline and maturity

---

16 I intentionally titled this section "God loves the marriage covenant" to distinguish from the thought that "God loves married people" or the incorrect implication that God loves married people more than single people. That is not true. Throughout church history, we have seen the rise and fall of Christians who have either elevated marriage or elevated singleness. I believe that some Christian cultures in the United States idolize marriage, and that is sinful. The results can particularly put a burden and identity crisis on God's daughters who may be single but desire marriage, who have the gift of singleness, who have elected to live a celibate lifestyle, or who are widowed and remain unmarried. The Bible is clear that choosing singleness is a good choice and marriage is also good. The Bible is also clear that the call to marriage can be a challenging ministry and responsibility to sustain over time, and if a person thinks that marriage is too difficult of a ministry assignment (as it cannot simply be a lustful decision), then it is best if that person remains single (Matthew 19:10–12; 1 Corinthians 7).

17 Also see Deuteronomy 22:13–27; Matthew 19:1–9; and 1 Corinthians 6:9–11.

that God is asking *all* believers to exercise within ourselves when loving our neighbors and honoring their bodies. In Matthew 5:29–30, Jesus used hyperbole to reinforce the seriousness of sin. He is not calling for the maiming of one's body; instead, He is calling His hearers to self-discipline regarding their eyes, hands, and any body part that causes them to sin. The Bible says that our bodies are structures for the Holy Spirit, and we do not belong to ourselves. Therefore, we are to honor God with our bodies (1 Corinthians 6:12–20).

The other reason God loves marriage is because it is a covenant that reveals His heart of sacrificial and selfless love, and it is a metaphor reflecting God's relationship with His people—first Israel, then His New Testament church. "The analogy between marriage and the relationship between God and His people speaks of monogamy. God did not bind himself to many, but to Israel alone."[18] Marriage calls us to undivided devotion to God first, and then to one spouse above all other human connections (2 Corinthians 11:1–3). Jesus taught: "At the beginning the Creator 'made them male and female,' and said, 'For this reason a man will leave his father and mother and be united to his wife, and the two will become one flesh'" (Matthew 19:4–5).

> **Adultery in marriage is idolatry in worship.**

Our monogamous marriages can bear witness to the love, mutual submission, holiness, unity, and oneness that we share with Jesus Christ (Ephesians 5:21–33). Adultery is a breach of the marital covenant for which God allows divorce.[19] Adultery in marriage is idolatry in worship. "Therefore what God has joined together, let no one separate" (Matthew 19:6).

---

18 Bockmuehl, *The Christian Way of Living*, 104.
19 Matthew 5:31–32 and 19:1–9; 1 Corinthians 7. Just because adultery permits divorce does *not* necessarily mean that someone should run to divorce court. These are matters of the heart in which a believer has the opportunity to confess and repent of their sins (meaning that they do not continue in the same sinful practices).

Question

How do you show love, honor, and appreciation to the people and relationships that God has placed in your life?

Day 5

God Loves When His People Flourish

SCRIPTURE READING
Exodus 20:15–17

SUPPLEMENTAL READING
Deuteronomy 5:19–21

There are many ways to love our neighbors and build each other up. In God's good economy—if we are physically able and if there is opportunity—we build each other up by working to provide for ourselves so as not to steal or become a burden to our neighbors. We also build each other up by creating boundaries for a safe community, by telling the truth, being trustworthy witnesses, and not coveting our neighbor's blessings.

God Loves Work and Its Provision

"You shall not steal" (Exodus 20:15; Deuteronomy 5:19; also see Leviticus 19:11). Leviticus 19:13 reveals that stealing is an injustice against one's neighbor, robbing them of what is rightfully theirs: their time, talents, and treasures. Leviticus expands the meaning of this commandment: "Do not defraud or rob your neighbor. Do not hold back the wages of a hired worker overnight." Stealing is when a child intentionally takes and does not return their teacher's pencil, or lifts a bicycle from the garage down the street, only to sell the parts at the local pawnshop. Adults steal too. This commandment is to any employer who has decision-making authority for hiring and salaries. As God's people, we must not exploit or rob our neighbors.

Sometimes adults steal because they are irresponsible or lack the tools and resources needed to flourish in life. Adult stealing includes not paying what you owe on taxes, taking company supplies for personal use, or delaying payments when your bills are due. It includes logging hours that you do not work, or *not* giving your best at work. Some steal because they are greedy and unjust, and dehumanize their neighbors, specifically the poor, women, minorities, and vulnerable people groups.

Stealing leads to inequitable practices. According to the US Department of Labor and the 2020 Bureau of Labor Statistics data, women earn eighty-two cents for every dollar that a man makes.[20] That number decreases when race is a factor. Stealing is consistently working part-time or hourly employees right up to the threshold of what would be considered full-time employment, or paying contracted workers under the table either because we are consciously underpaying or because we don't want to offer benefits packages. We steal when we don't pay workers overtime. The Bible speaks extensively about God's displeasure with the injustices of greed and exploitation, especially when it is done to our poor neighbors.[21]

Some people steal because they lack the discipline, desire, or opportunity to work. Working is a part of our creative calling from the beginning (Genesis 2:4–7). It is one of the ways we image God. As a result of the fall, our work can be difficult (3:17–19). Sometimes our hard work does not yield results, so we succumb to slothfulness or stealing from our neighbors. All able-bodied adults should work to enhance their families and

---

20 Janelle Jones, "5 Facts about the State of the Gender Pay Gap," US Department of Labor, March 19, 2021, https://blog.dol.gov/2021/03/19/5-facts-about-the-state-of-the-gender-pay-gap.

21 Some references: Isaiah 58:3–6; Proverbs 22:16, 22–23; Psalms 35:10; 73.

communities. Whenever we allow able-bodied adults to sit in our residences and not work or contribute in some way, we are condoning the sin of their idleness, and are turning them into thieves under our own roofs. That makes us complicit in their sin. Paul was a bi-vocational minister. He worked as a tentmaker to support his missional work. Read what he wrote in 2 Thessalonians 3:6–13.

Paul revealed that his work offered provision to meet his basic needs. He also shared that keeping company with idle people could corrupt the community. "Do not be misled: 'Bad company corrupts good character'" (1 Corinthians 15:33). We are to work and set a good example for our neighbors to emulate because idleness can lead to foolishness and disruption, thereby destroying the community. We know that in the communities where unemployment or underemployment is high, crime and violence are also high. Therefore, it is good for people to work and to provide for themselves and their families, so as not to burden their neighbors.

God Is a Lover of Truth

"You shall not give false testimony against your neighbor" (Exodus 20:16; Deuteronomy 5:20). Leviticus 19:11 and 16 reads: "Do not lie. Do not deceive one another. . . . Do not go about spreading slander among your people. Do not do anything that endangers your neighbor's life. I am the LORD." This commandment directly connects to several others, specifically the third commandment about swearing. Remember, the commandments are for civil use, determining what makes their society just. So, if people are lying, gossiping, or bearing false witness against their neighbor, especially regarding a civil or judicial dispute like murder or adultery, that lie could lead to their neighbor's untimely death. In this and all matters, the positive response is to tell the truth instead of manipulating, embellishing, or lying about a situation (Leviticus 19:17), especially when under oath.[22]

---

22   Reference Exodus 23:1–3, 6–8; Matthew 5:33–37; and Leviticus 19:15.

Get straight to the point, for "when there are many words, wrongdoing is unavoidable, but one who restrains his lips is wise" (Proverbs 10:19 NASB).

God desires for His people to act in integrity, to become a community of neighbors who do and mean what they say. Truth-telling builds trust among neighbors and creates an environment of safety and security within a society. It communicates to a watching world that we are God's *holy* people (Colossians 3:9–10).

God Loves Our Neighbors

God loves when our neighbors flourish. "You shall not covet your neighbor's house . . . your neighbor's wife, or his male or female servant, his ox or donkey, or anything that belongs to your neighbor" (Exodus 20:17; also see Deuteronomy 5:21). "The Hebrew word for covet is the verb 'chamad' and 'awah', which connote a strong desire and possessiveness."[23] Coveting can lead to sin because the thing that we want doesn't belong to us. Coveting your neighbor's house could lead to stealing. Coveting your neighbor's wife could lead to adultery. Coveting your neighbor's source of income could lead to slander, blackmail, or worse. Coveting and jealousy are two sides of the same coin. Coveting is a heart issue that can destroy relationships. We know from James 4:1–3 that an unchecked heart regarding this issue can lead to violence. Coveting feeds the devil's lie that God is withholding His best from us (Genesis 3:1, 4–5). Sometimes God constrains a perceived "blessing" because He knows we can't handle it. If a "blessing" takes us away from delighting in the Lord (Psalm 37:4), that is not medicine for our ailing hearts. Coveting can lead to addiction. The social media dilemma[24] reveals the dangers that occur when companies spend billions in marketing to partner with platforms to influence our thoughts, compromise our values, and entice us into buying things we do not need.

---

23   Klaus Bockmuehl, *The Christian Way of Living: An Ethics of the Ten Commandments* (Vancouver, British Columbia: Regent College Publishing, 1994), 121.

24   View *The Social Dilemma*, Jeff Orlowski's 2020 documentary, on Netflix.

We have become a culture of social media addicts where "likes" turn into an evaluation of our worth leading to depression and even suicide.[25] The "reality" of social media tells us that someone else always has what we want or lack, so our desires increase. When we can't acquire the desire, a spiritual war wages inwardly. We become jealous; we may get angry. This proves that the idol is in our lives (Ephesians 5:5; Colossians 3:15), and our motives are wrong.

Coveting is not just about what we can buy; it is also about our posture toward God and how we define our *being*. When we covet, we are expressing an attitude of ungratefulness for what God has provided. We have been bamboozled to think that having more accomplishments, more stuff, or cooler friends will make us feel better about ourselves, but we don't have to look far to recount tragedies of celebrities and privileged people who have all the things that we covet but are still unhappy, drowning their sorrows in a bottle, drugs, and sex, because outside trappings will never cover our emptiness or brokenness. We need Jesus Christ to save us from ourselves and the Holy Spirit to do a work *in* us so we can respond like Paul: "I have learned to be content whatever the circumstances. . . . I have learned the secret of being content in any and every situation, whether well fed or hungry, whether living in plenty or in want" (Philippians 4:11–12). Learning contentment and our human value apart from the outside trappings and maintaining a grateful heart are the disciplined actions that kill the demand to covet.

Finally, coveting is about how we relate to our neighbors' blessings. If our neighbor has a new car or a significant social media following or goes on a nice vacation, their spouse gets promoted, or their child gets accepted into a top-notch school, then we can become jealous because we want their life. Let's consider: *Why can't we be happy for our neighbors when God blesses them?* God is not short on supply and God loves when *all* his

---

25 US Senate Committee on Commerce, Science, and Transportation, "Protecting Kids Online: Testimony from a Facebook Whistleblower," October 5, 2021, https://www.commerce.senate.gov/2021/10/protecting%20kids%20online:%20testimony%20from%20a%20facebook%20whistleblower.

people flourish! When God blesses our neighbors with wealth, success, good health, clean skin, great relationships, new clothes, and influence, being a good neighbor means that we celebrate. We worship and thank God, knowing that the blessing is right down the street and, at the opportune time, God will also bless us. A home improvement project in my neighborhood can increase my property value. If someone else's child or spouse flourishes, that

> **Why can't we be happy for our neighbors when God blesses them?**

can motivate my family. I can be inspired by my neighbors whom God is blessing and learn from them if I am not jealous or posing a threat by coveting their stuff.

This sin is an easy trap to fall into especially when we scroll social media daily. I take seriously my responsibility as a writer, and my book sales don't always reflect the commitment or quality of my work. So, when I see other people's books being recommended, become aware of their sales numbers, or see their Amazon reviews, I can become discouraged on a good day and jealous on my worst. When this happens, I sometimes stop to pray for the author, their family, ministry, and book projects. I pray for God to continue to bless them and enlarge their territory. This prayer changes my heart concerning the matter because it shifts my attention back to God and reminds me that God is not short on His reserves, that I am genuinely happy when God uses my sister or brother to send His Word forth, and that they are obedient to the work. Praying also expresses my gratitude that God has also called and is indeed using me. Prayer doesn't change the reality of the situation, but it does change the condition of my heart. In which case, I flourish too by growing more in love with God, affirming my identity in Christ alone, and loving my neighbor.

Questions

In what areas are you most tempted to neglect your love of neighbors?

In what areas are you most encouraged to bless your neighbors and celebrate their flourishing?

Weekend Reflection

God Has the Right Perspective

SCRIPTURE READING
Psalm 119

God is preparing His people for a destination and a future. The wilderness provides a landscape for that preparation. "The wilderness is where people start building for the place they are going, and for that they need the right perspective."[26] The purpose of the Ten Commandments is to give the right perspective about Israel's relationship with God and their neighbors. It presents God's standard for love for the purpose of shaping Israel into a unified and holy community that represents God to a watching world. God already established Israel as His chosen people, so the law was to discipline them to respond out of their true identity.

> Unlike manna, which normally provided physical nourishment only for one day, God's word would sustain them

---

26 Natasha Sistrunk Robinson, *A Sojourner's Truth: Choosing Freedom and Courage in a Divided World* (Downers Grove, IL: InterVarsity Press, 2018), 155.

for a lifetime. This food, which they would come to know as "the law," was as important to them as the air they breathed because it taught them how to live as holy people before God. As Timothy Laniak wrote, "The most significant 'food' in the wilderness was the Law itself." . . .

The law was an expression of God's grace to a broken people, and it served as part of his redemptive plan so the Israelites could learn how to live holy lives that were acceptable and pleasing to him. . . .

The Ten Commandments served to guide and set apart the Israelites while preserving the greatest good for all. On numerous occasions, God instructed the Israelites to love and teach this law to the sojourners and aliens living among them, and to treat them as native born because God does not show partiality (see Leviticus 19:33–34; Deuteronomy 10:17–19). God gave this instruction because he was building a new community of people who would live fully devoted to him. If everyone—young and old, female and male, Jew and Gentile, slave and free—obeyed the law to love God (as the first three commandments require) and to love their neighbor (as the remaining seven indicate), it would make for a better society.

Natasha Sistrunk Robinson, *A Sojourner's Truth*

Group Discussion

1. What is the purpose of the Decalogue?

2. How can you encourage yourself in faithful daily actions, understanding that the promises and blessings of God can leave a legacy for thousands of generations?

3. What are some ways that idol worship subtly creeps into your life, and what can you do to reject these temptations?

4. How does God's love inform your love of self and love of neighbor?

5. Which one of the Ten Commandments has convicted or ministered to you most deeply in this season in your life, and why?

_____

_____

_____

_____

_____

_____

_____

_____

_____

_____

_____

_____

_____

_____

_____

_____

_____

Creating a
Just Society

"For my thoughts are not your thoughts,
neither are your ways my ways," declares
the Lord. *"As the heavens are higher than*
the earth, so are my ways higher than your
ways and my thoughts than your thoughts."

Isaiah 55:8–9

Day 1

Commentary

Exodus 21–24 reveal what it looks like for Israel to live as a just society:

> Justice in the Bible is the act of restoring community and healing broken relationships. . . . Biblical justice (*tsedeqah, mishpat, dikaiosune*) focuses on the widow, the orphan, the poor, the outsiders, and rejected ones and calls the rich and powerful to cease their domination and be generously reconciled with those they have exploited. . . . Justice also relates to God's desire to liberate all of humanity from sin.[1]

When speaking about justice within Christian circles, I have made a habit of referencing "biblical justice" instead of "social justice." I've conditioned myself to respond this way to assure mostly White evangelical audiences that I am deeply committed to the Bible, that I am *not* teaching a "different" gospel other than the gospel of Jesus Christ, and that I don't have some hidden agenda. I have also done this with the awareness of power dynamics and gatekeepers within Western Christendom.

---

1   Bruce Demarest and Keith J. Matthews, eds., *Dictionary of Everyday Theology and Culture* (Colorado Springs, CO: NavPress, 2010), 240.

The justice debate is mostly crafted by White+male+evangelicals. History has shown that this group has a track record of not advocating for vulnerable women or children when they are preyed upon by powerful men in the church, will only selectively uphold the standards of personal piety with regard to the male (because they are always a male) political candidates they support, and has intentionally switched the focus of an important national conversation about the value of Black lives and the history of systemic racism in the United States. Therefore, I cannot write about justice with integrity without also acknowledging the injustice of these sins within our society and the church in the United States.

Having grown up in the Black Church, I understand that there is no distinction between biblical and social justice for many Black Christians who are pursuing righteousness in their communities because of the example of Jesus.[2] The purpose of politics is to make laws and set boundaries to ensure a safe and thriving society. Therefore, some Black Christians "lean left" politically because they are motivated out of love for their neighbors, not because they disregard the Bible or God's holiness. Embodying our theology is just and redemptive work.

God communicates to Israel about becoming a holy people—exemplars for watching nations—and He does so by establishing standards of justice within the context of the social systems in which they already live. In his book *Generous Justice*, Dr. Timothy Keller wrote, "Israel was charged to create a culture of social justice for the poor and vulnerable because it was the way the nation could reveal God's glory and character to the world."[3] Injustice yields violence, poverty, and the abuse of power. Before providing commandments, God is ensuring that His just laws are enforced in the same way for everyone. The Bible often uses the words "justice" (Hebrew word *mishpat*) and "righteousness" (Hebrew term *tzadeqah*) together. "The word . . . *tzadeqah* . . . refers to a life of right

---

2   Reference Matthew 5:1–12; 25:31–46; and Luke 4:14–21.
3   Timothy Keller, *Generous Justice: How God's Grace Makes Us Just* (New York: Penguin Group, 2010), 9.

relationships. . . . This means . . . that Biblical righteousness is inevitably 'social,' because it is about relationships."[4] Righteousness is not just what we pursue politically in the public square; it is also what we display in our personal interactions with others. "In the Bible *tzadeqah* refers to day-to-day living in which a person conducts *all* relationships in family and society with fairness, generosity, and equity."[5] When asking the question, "What does the LORD require of you [His people]," the prophet Micah wrote, "To act justly and to love mercy and to walk humbly with your God" (Micah 6:8). We grant our neighbors mercy because God has been merciful to us. God does not treat us as our sins deserve (Psalm 103:6–14); otherwise, we would all be physically *and* spiritually dead with no hope of life, help, or salvation. We respond in humility, understanding that only God makes us just. God is establishing right relationships within the community by training Israel to issue judgments with fairness (everyone gets the same punishments for the same crimes), to give people what they are rightfully due (e.g., by ensuring that the basic needs of Maslow's hierarchy are met within the community), to practice the Golden Rule, and to offer restitution for those harmed in society.

Patriarchy in the World and the Bible

The biblical world we have entered, and the world in which many of us still live, is a patriarchal society. While our society has evolved concerning women's rights, inequality is prevalent when we ponder issues like pay equity, leadership (e.g., consider the US presidency or senior positions in any public domain), or who has the ability to build wealth. Our society benefits men. However, the patriarchy that we observe today is *not* the same as the patriarchy experienced in the Bible. "All forms of patriarchy are not equally bad—patriarchy is a continuum."[6] Understanding patriarchy

---

4   Keller, *Generous Justice*, 10.
5   Keller, 10.
6   Carolyn Custis James, *Malestrom: Manhood Swept into the Currents of a Changing World* (Grand Rapids, MI: Zondervan, 2015), 30.

as a continuum helps us better interpret the weight of God's law and the justice He offers. On this topic, Carolyn Custis James wrote:

> Patriarchy matters because it is the cultural backdrop of the Bible. . . . Patriarchy matters because the prevalence of this cultural system on the pages of Scripture, in cultures around the world, and throughout history can easily lead (and has led) to the assumption that patriarchy is divinely ordained. . . .
>
> It is *not* the Bible's message, but a teaching tool God has chosen to open our eyes to the "not of this world" nature of the kingdom of heaven of which we are citizens.[7]

So, what is it? The first female minister to be ordained by a Dutch Reformed Mission Church in South Africa, Rev. Prof. Dr. Mary-Anne Plaatjies van Huffel wrote:

> Patriarchy is a social system that promotes hierarchies and awards economic, political and social power to one group over others. . . . Classical patriarchy refers to the domination of the male over the female, children, servants and slaves. . . . Patriarchy also refers to structures and ideologies which engender the domination and exploitation of the weak and the powerless amongst us. Therefore patriarchy can rightly be described as empire, a *spirit of lordless domination, created by humankind.*[8]

This brief reflection reveals: (1) patriarchy is an earthly social system that was set up by fallen humans, not God; (2) when carried to its full extent

---

7   James, *Malestrom*, 31, 57.
8   Mary-Anne Plaatjies van Huffel, "Patriarchy as Empire: A Theological Reflection," *Studia Historiae Ecclesiasticae* 37, no. S1 (December 2011), 259–70.

and classical understanding, patriarchy creates division (between women and men, and strife amongst men), so it does not promote unity amongst neighbors, and (3) within the Bible, patriarchy defines the kingdoms of this world (e.g., Egypt, Babylon, Rome, the United States) in contrast to the kingdom of God. This is the political, social, and theological reality of patriarchy.

Why do we care? Hermeneutics demands proper context. If we read our cultural understanding *into* the text, we risk misinterpretation and can incorrectly conclude that God's solutions are also unjust. Within patriarchy, "might" leads to the assumption that maleness is "right." That assumption often leads to violence and the abuse of power. God restrains patriarchy by enforcing the male's societal responsibility, then the Father sent Jesus as the epitome of manhood. Jesus's ministry and kingdom offer a better way for us all. Justice and righteousness—not sex or gender—rule supreme in God's kingdom.

Question

What are your reflections on the social system of patriarchy and the concept of justice?

Day 2

Slavery and
Personal Injury

SCRIPTURE READING
Exodus 21

My psyche cannot forget the reports read, firsthand accounts heard, documentaries and undercover investigations watched about slavery. Slavery is a vicious, dark evil, and remembering motivates me to fight for justice. Regarding the laws about slavery and personal injury, God calls Israel to remember that they were once slaves in Egypt.

The Transatlantic Slave Trade

I am a descendant of the Transatlantic Slave Trade and I have been an advocate against modern-day slavery or human trafficking. It is not lost on me that descendants of the Transatlantic Slave Trade continue to fight for the dignity and justice of Black lives today, while most of the advocates that I have encountered in the fight against modern-day slavery are White people. These two communities of justice seekers rarely interact. Both systems of slavery are complex, and it might help us better understand God's desire for justice if we understood the roots of slavery.

The Transatlantic Slave Trade was motivated by White greed and capitalism, imposed on Black bodies from several countries in West Africa, and justified by the social construct of race. The only way to rationalize this inhuman treatment of humans made in the image of God is by crafting narratives that defined them as subhuman. Quoting the founding fathers of the United States, Rev. Dr. Kelly Brown Douglas addresses their distorted theological imagination when she wrote about this problem:

> In America the principal conception of the black body is as chattel. . . . First and foremost, to be chattel meant that black people did not have the rights to possess their bodies. They did not own them. Neither did they have the right to possess other black bodies, not even those of their children. In this regard, the chatteled black body is not cherished property. It is instead a valued commodity. . . . The black body as chattel is essentially the valued commodity of whiteness. . . . The more labor that chattel can produce, then the more valued a commodity that chattel is. This is why healthy young black men and fertile young black women were sold for top dollar at slave auctions.[9]

This is the foundation of the political and judicial system that shaped the psyche of the White male founders of the United States, and continually creates a social predicament. Douglas continues: "To characterize black people as chattel is to define them as quintessentially belonging to another. Blackness becomes virtually a synonym for enslavement. Freedom is not a right that black women and men are entitled to by their very chattel condition."[10] If we chart American history from the enslavement of free Black Africans to the mass incarceration of Black bodies that Dr. Michelle Alexander calls "the

---

9   Kelly Brown Douglas, *Stand Your Ground: Black Bodies and the Justice of God* (Maryknoll, NY: Orbis Books, 2015), 52–54.
10   Douglas, *Stand Your Ground*, 55.

New Jim Crow," we witness a fundamental problem concerning the United States' distorted view of Black people, Black bodies, and our work.

This is a political, social, and theological problem where White men have exercised their power and privilege to define "God's natural law." English philosopher John Locke wrote about property and the interpretation of natural rights in his *Second Treatise of Government*. He indicated that "every man has a property in his own person," and a man had the right to the labor of his own body and work, only *if* they had the right to their personhood.[11] The conclusion: free people had rights to their own bodies and labor, and enslaved people did not. Douglas wrote that Locke's treatise informed the framers of the Declaration of Independence. Herein lies the problem with chattel slavery: "If God's eternal law is discerned through nature itself, in this instance through the way the world is, then the way things are can easily be construed as the way things are supposed to be. . . . Natural law theory in the hands of subjugating power can become a dangerous tool. For it serves to justify unjust structures, and thus it sanctifies an oppressive status quo."[12]

And there is more. Dr. Tony Evans wrote:

> The American myth of the inferior nature of African people began when the European slave traders subjugated Africans and exported them to the New World. . . . Because the slave trade was so extensive and because so many of its promulgators claimed to be Christians, [a] religious justification had to be promoted with as little resistance as possible. And the myth of inferiority had to be valid in the minds of the slaves as well as in the minds of the white traders so they would accept it as natural.[13]

---

11 John Locke, *Two Treatises of Government* 2.5.27, Project Gutenberg, accessed December 8, 2021, https://gutenberg.org/cache/epub/7370/pg7370-images.html. Originally published 1689.

12 Douglas, *Stand Your Ground*, 56.

13 Tony Evans, *Oneness Embraced through the Eyes of Tony Evans: A Fresh Look at Reconciliation, the Kingdom, and Justice* (Chicago: Moody Publishers, 2011), 90–91.

With the approval of the Roman Catholic Church, there was an "evangelistic" motivation to human enslavement.[14] "Because many Christians presumed that paganism was inherently part of the African's religion,[15] they looked to the Bible . . . to authenticate the slave industry. . . . This set the stage for the infamous 'curse of Ham' doctrine."[16] This theology taught that as a result of Genesis 9:18–26, Noah's son, Ham, and his descendants (the Canaanites) were cursed to perpetually live as enslaved beings . . . The Old Scofield Reference Bible endorsed the "curse of Ham" theory.[17]

Modern-Day Slavery

Unlike the Transatlantic Slave Trade, modern-day slavery[18] is not motivated by the social construct or a distorted theology about Black inferiority. However, it is motivated by greed and is just as deadly, deceptive, and evil. At its core, there is a twisted view about humanity and the will of God for some humans. "Human trafficking is a form of modern-day slavery in which traffickers use force, fraud, or coercion to control victims for the purpose of engaging in commercial sex acts or labor services against his/her will."[19] This form of slavery *can* include various methods of inhuman treatment like separation from family, starvation or the rationing

---

14   For more on this, I recommend reading Kelly Brown Douglas's book *Stand Your Ground: Black Bodies and the Justice of God* and Mark Charles and Soong-Chan Rah's book, *Unsettling Truths: The Ongoing, Dehumanizing Legacy of the Doctrine of Discovery.*

15   This too is a myth. Recommended reading includes Philip Jenkins, *The Lost History of Christianity: The Thousand-Year Golden Age of the Church in the Middle East, Africa, and Asia—and How It Died,* and *History of Eastern Christianity* by Aziz S. Atiya, or if you want something lighter or less scholarly, look at Thomas C. Oden's *How Africa Shaped the Christian Mind: Rediscovering the African Seedbed of Western Christianity.*

16   Evans, *Oneness Embraced,* 92.

17   Evans, 92–93.

18   According to the State Department, "Human trafficking can include, but does not require, movement. People may be considered trafficking victims regardless of whether they were born into a state of servitude, were exploited in their home town, were transported to the exploitative situation, previously consented to work for a trafficker, or participated in a crime as a direct result of being trafficked. At the heart of this phenomenon is the traffickers' aim to exploit and enslave their victims and the myriad coercive and deceptive practices they use to do so." US Department of State, "What Is Modern Slavery?," accessed December 8, 2021, https://www.state.gov/what-is-modern-slavery/.

19   National Human Trafficking Hotline, "Human Trafficking," accessed December 8, 2021, https://human traffickinghotline.org/type-trafficking/human-trafficking. This national hotline,1-888-373-7888, is operated by Polaris Project.

of meals, doping, or violence like beatings and rape. Both forms of slavery can occur as a result of kidnapping, which Exodus 21:16 explicitly forbids. In God's good society, kidnapping, especially for the purpose of enslavement, is punishable by death.

While I'm no longer as active of an advocate in the anti–human trafficking movement, I have spent many years praying, fundraising, lobbying, leading book discussions, giving philanthropically, hosting and supporting educational events nationally and within my local community. According to the End It Movement, there are still more than 40.3 million enslaved people throughout the world, with 71 percent of them being women and girls, and one in four victims being children.[20]

Modern-day slavery takes on many forms, and although it is illegal in *every* country in the world, it is also prevalent everywhere. It includes sex slavery, with which some people are familiar, though I suspect folks don't understand the gravity of this darkness. I have watched undercover investigation videos of brothels where rich and powerful men come from across the world to countries like Thailand, where they can purchase sex with little girls as young as four years old with discretion and impunity, and others where similar abusers can access the pornography of children in the Philippines from the privacy of their own homes. The darkness is worse than any decent human can stomach. Modern-day slavery also includes forced labor where people are made to lay bricks in India or little boys are forced to work in the fishing industry or drown in Ghana's Lake Volta. It includes humans who are wasting away while sewing (so we can wear cheap clothes), cutting cocoa trees (to produce chocolate 's not fair trade), or mining (so we can access oil). It also includes ·itude and the recruitment and use of child soldiers. I am ⁺ tions like the International Justice Mission (IJM). ·

---

20 End It Movement, "Slavery by the Numbers," accessed ·
   This is the estimated number based on known inform·
   victims are hidden in plain sight, so the reality of th

Relief, World Vision, The Salvation Army, and Polaris Project that work aggressively to educate and end this injustice throughout the world.[21]

Slavery in the Bible

What we understand historically and socially about the Transatlantic Slave Trade and modern-day slavery is different than the slavery we see in Exodus 21. While I take some solace in knowing that slavery in the Bible was not motivated by the social construct of race, I hate the institution of slavery in any form. It troubles me deeply that God didn't abolish it altogether. While this is my honest belief, this confession is also steeped in pride. What do I, a mere human, know about God's infinite understanding? Notwithstanding slavery and its various practices, God's law in Exodus 21 ensures the fair treatment of slaves. Slavery in the Ancient Near East was normally a result of war (i.e., citizens of losing kingdoms could become slaves of winning kingdoms) or poverty (e.g., people could sell themselves or their family members into slavery to settle a debt). Concerning the latter, slavery in Exodus 21 was more like indentured servitude where citizens could work off debt and this allowed for their survival.

Exodus reveals that Hebrews were *selling themselves to their own people.* Today, poor families can be enslaved when they are offered a loan (without business acumen or legal counsel), and are charged astronomical amounts of interest that they can never repay, so they are enslaved indefinitely.

Within God's just society, humans could not be enslaved indefinitely. God put a maximum limit of six years on a business contract between the master and slave. Whether the debt is paid or not, God says that the slave *must* go free in the seventh year. If the slave came to his master with a wife, then he and his wife must go free in the seventh year.

ducated and become a more just consumer, I encourage you to check out Fair Trade USA
usa.org), the Rainforest Alliance (www.rainforest-alliance.org), Made in a Free World
ld.org), and Not for Sale (www.notforsalecampaign.org).

Throughout history, poverty serves as the catalyst leading to slavery. Vulnerable people can sell themselves, their children, or their entire family into slavery to avoid starvation or to pay a debt. People who owe debts should pay them. Justice also requires that borrowers know what they are agreeing to so they can consider the real cost, and that lenders offer loans at a fair price without consuming interest (making a person's bad financial situation worse).

God wants His people to have a higher responsibility to those within their community. We see this in Exodus 22:25: "If you lend money to one of my people among you who is needy, do not treat it like a business deal; charge no interest." God also desires that the poor people and the aliens or foreigners within their society are protected, and not exploited. Read Leviticus 25:35–43.

Even with these restrictions, slavery was a reality of life in the Bible. The whole system is problematic because it gives humans the "rights of ownership" over other humans. This problem is evident in Exodus 21:4–6, where the master "gifts" his female slave to a male slave. Despite marriage, the wife *and* her offspring belong to the master even if the male slave is freed. This is where Dr. Douglas's statement about "valued commodity" informs our understanding. The wife and her children have more value to the master, especially if she is in her childbearing years and the children are healthy enough to work. In Genesis 16:1–9, the enslaved Hagar was raped by her master, Abram, at the command of his barren wife, Sarai. Once conceived, Hagar's son belonged to her master, Sarai, not his biological mother. If the male slave in Exodus 21 wanted to remain with his family, then his *only* choice was to denounce his freedom, declare his love for his master, and then go before the judges to make his enslavement permanent. This declaration was accomplished by an ear piercing (a form of branding) indicating his master's permanent ownership over him.

Within the context of patriarchy, Exodus 21:7–11 provides protection for a woman who had no agency, especially if she came from an impoverished family. Her protection and provisions were directly connected to the men in her life. If her father could not provide for her, he had the option of selling her into slavery, thereby ensuring her provisions. That's why she is not to "go free" even if her master is not pleased with her. Where else would she go? If her master decided to "gift" her to his son, then he must grant her the full rights of being his daughter. Within a just society, whether the master keeps the enslaved woman for himself or his son, he must continue to provide her with food, clothing, and marital rights. She could be freed only if the master failed to provide her with these three things.

Several personal injuries are presented in Exodus 21. The violence of slavery rears its ugly head again in verses 20 and 21: "Anyone who beats their male or female slave with a rod must be punished if the slave dies as a direct result, but they are not to be punished if the slave recovers after a day or two, since the slave is their property." If the master is so violent as to cause bodily injury to their slave, then the slave must be granted his or her freedom (vv. 26–27). Ultimately, what we see in this chapter is God providing some protections within the social system of slavery.

Question

How does the context of slavery discussed in this week inform your understanding of the law?

Day 3

Social Responsibility

SCRIPTURE READING
Exodus 22

Chapter 22 reminds us that the laws "were intended to form Israel into a community that lived in keeping with God's way of justice and righteousness. They spelled out in specific ways how God's people could use the power God had given them to seek the flourishing of everyone in their midst."[22] Communal flourishing is anchored in God's command to love one's neighbors. It requires a respect for God's laws which govern the land, and a mutual respect for a neighbor's property and relationships. Healthy relationships and healthy boundaries provide safety and security, which build communal trust, and are essential aspects of a flourishing society.

Beginning with the laws about protection of a neighbor's property, "Scripture . . . shows that God's invitation and call to justice isn't just an individual concern, but that it speaks to society."[23] Exodus 22:1–15 revisits the commandment, "Do not steal." God's law required that any thief found guilty of stealing take social responsibility and make restitution (vv. 1, 3–7, 9, 12). Restitution is "the act or condition of restoring something to its

---

22 Bethany Hanke Hoang and Kristen Deede Johnson, *The Justice Calling: Where Passion Meets Perseverance* (Grand Rapids, MI: Brazos Press, 2016), 92.
23 Bruce Demarest and Keith J. Matthews, eds., *Dictionary of Everyday Theology and Culture* (Colorado Springs, CO: NavPress, 2010), 241.

rightful owner, making good of or giving an equivalent for some injury; or a legal action serving to cause restoration of a previous state."[24] God required the thief to return what they stole with interest (i.e., we might consider this a "restitution tax" due to the injured party). If the thief couldn't make restitution, they could be sold into slavery to pay off the debt accrued because of their theft (v. 3). There is no God-endorsed example in the Bible where people stole and were continually allowed to reap the benefits of their thievery! Here lies again the biblical case for reparations.

Showing respect for a neighbor's personal property also included taking responsibility for neglect and providing restitution for destroying anything (property or animal) that doesn't belong to you (vv. 6, 10–15). These laws confirmed that the protection and care of one's land and animals directly impacted the ability for a man to provide for his family. The Israelites lived in an agricultural society and some of them were shepherds by trade. Their animals were not pets. Animals provided transportation, milk, meat for sacrifices or eating, and they plowed the land for gardening. The produce from such harvests had the ability to feed several families for a season, so losing one's animal or property/land was just like losing a job or income stream.

Social Relationships

The law continually provided protection for the most vulnerable—namely the poor, orphaned children, and *aliens*—and because of patriarchy, vulnerable populations also included women and widows. Concerning the poor, "these laws include regulations that ensure clothes used as collateral for a loan are given back before sundown so that everyone has a way to stay warm overnight, prohibitions against collecting interest on loans given to the poor, and guidelines for fair treatment in courts of law."[25] I hear God's compassion when I read statements like: "If you lend money to

---

24 *Merriam-Webster*, s.v. "restitution (n.)," accessed July 31, 2021, www.merriam-webster.com/dictionary /restitution.

25 Hoang and Johnson, *The Justice Calling*, 91.

one of my people among you who is needy, do not treat it like a business deal; charge no interest. If you take your neighbor's cloak as a pledge, return it by sunset, because that cloak is the only covering your neighbor has. What else can they sleep in?" (Exodus 22:25–27). God is concerned about the community meeting the needs of those who are impoverished among them. I lament because I know that too often our society exploits or ignores, rather than shows compassion to, our vulnerable populations. Our impoverished communities are littered with businesses like "payday loans," "same-day cash lending," and "car title exchange" schemes that are all intentionally designed to make an impoverished person's bad financial situation worse. The interest rates and terms of those arrangements should not legally be allowed. God says, "Give your neighbor what they need to get through the day. Don't you care whether they are safe and warm at night?" Then God warns the Israelites, "If you exploit or take advantage of the poor, and they cry out to me, I will hear them and show compassion, and God's wrath and judgment will fall on you" (see vv. 22–24, 27).

Additionally, God tells the Israelites not to mistreat or oppress the aliens[26] living among them (v. 21). Remember that other nations—perhaps some Egyptians—left with the Israelites. When citizens leave their country to sojourn in another place, they become vulnerable aliens who are without rights in a foreign land so they are at the mercy of their travel companions, especially if they are in need or if they get into trouble. God says, "Don't mistreat them."

This law reveals that there are two heart conditions to deal with: the Israelites' temptation to get revenge, and the Egyptians' fear of the formerly enslaved. The Egyptians lose power as they wander into the desert with the people who are no longer subservient to them. They know it, and perhaps the Israelites do too. What happens to the Egyptians as these

---

26 Some translations use "sojourner" or "foreigner." This group includes refugees or anyone who is not native to the occupied land.

power dynamics change? This question provides an opportunity for theological and social reflection. I believe part of the reason some White people don't want to have honest conversations about US history is because they will have to confront the lies we have all been taught. If they look at the darkness squarely, then they must consider the consequences of those actions. Deeper still is this underlying fear that if Black folks had ownership of their own bodies, work, land, businesses, and wealth—if equity was a reality—then that would be the demise of a society that has been centered around White dominance. The real fear of systemic Whiteness is: if given the opportunity, Black people will remember, gain power, and then treat White people the same way that White people have treated Black people. But there is a Word from the Lord. God says to the Israelites and to His Black children, "Don't treat them like they treat you."

Verses 16 and 17 reinforce the protection God provides for women within a patriarchal society. God says that a man (who has power and responsibility in society) who seduces and then has sex with a virgin (assuming consensual sex) should pay the bride-price and marry her, if her father approves. When I was growing up, women in my community would make statements like, "Why would a man buy the cow when he can get the milk for free?" These statements were meant to discourage young women like myself from giving ourselves to any man easily. We were encouraged to value ourselves enough to challenge a man to make a marital commitment and financial investment *before* having sex. This guidance may sound ridiculous in our "sexually liberated" society where fornication (sex outside of God's boundaries of marriage) is so prevalent. However, "there is nothing new under the sun" (Ecclesiastes 1:9). The Ancient Near East had many sexual revolutions of their own including bestiality (having sex with animals), for which God required death (Exodus 22:19). In these verses, however, God reveals that He values women, so He makes provision for the virgin's life.

God says to the man, "You are not to treat a woman in society as a prostitute. Make an honest woman out of her. If you are man enough to have sex with her, then be man enough to make her your wife, and take on the responsibility of supporting her financially." This might sound like a "barbaric" or "old-school" teaching, but it is quite gracious within the biblical context where arranged marriages were normal, and in a society where fornication could have ruined a woman's chance of marriage and a future. In this text, physical attraction is apparent between the two parties; however, this law is about financial provision for the virgin and her family given her compromised sexual condition.

The television network Lifetime has a series called *Married at First Sight*. I enjoy clips of it on occasion. When I first saw the show, I told my husband, "These are arranged marriages," which are still prevalent and normal in some Eastern cultures. In the West, however, we encourage people to marry for what we emotionally define as love although our divorce rates do not indicate that our approach to marriage is better. While the US divorce rate hit an all-time low in 2020, there has also been a decline in the number of marriages. According to Dr. Wendy Wang, director of research for the Institute for Family Studies:

> College-educated and economically better off Americans are more likely to marry and stay married, but working-class and poor Americans face more family instability and higher levels of singleness. For Americans in the top third income bracket, 64% are in an intact marriage, meaning they have only married once and are still in their first marriage. In contrast, only 24% of Americans in the lower-third income bracket are in an intact marriage [according to analysis of the 2018 census data]. . . .
>
> With the rates of both divorce and marriage dropping in America, we expect to see the marriage divide deepen and poor and working-class Americans increasingly

disconnected from the institution of marriage. The impact of this disconnection on our family lives can be destructive, which makes it an issue that policymakers, community leaders, and scholars should continue to pay attention to.[27]

I raise this issue because the institution of marriage, and the success or dissolution of it, has a direct impact on a person's financial situation. This is what God is addressing in the Scripture. The bride-price (*mohar*) is different than a dowry, because it is paid by the groom's family to the bride's father to honor the value of the bride and the work that she will contribute to the home. Once a woman was no longer a virgin, her father could not require a premium bride-price, so the man who seduced her was required to pay her father the bride-price, regardless of whether her father allowed a marriage to ensue. If her father did not believe that the man could provide for his daughter, then he could keep the bride-price *and* use it to provide for her. God is a good Father who provides for all His children, even His daughters.

Exercise

Take time to journal this week answering the question, "What makes a just society?" Prepare to share with your small group if possible.

27　Wendy Wang, "The U.S. Divorce Rate Has Hit a 50-Year Low," Institute for Family Studies, November 10, 2020, https://ifstudies.org/blog/the-us-divorce-rate-has-hit-a-50-year-low.

Day 4

Feasting with God

SCRIPTURE READING
Exodus 23

SUPPLEMENTAL READING
Leviticus 23; Numbers 29; Deuteronomy 16

It's tempting to skim through chapter 23 and ask, "Isn't this redundant?" To which I would reply, "Yes, it is." Repetition lets us know what's important. The Scriptures that we are privileged to read began as oral teachings, and the primary method for the community to learn God's ways was through repetition. God is preparing His people to go somewhere. Embrace the fact that God promised the Israelites prosperity, and told them that the promised land is bountiful. By providing festival instructions, God is saying to the people, "When you get over there to experience the place that overflows with milk and honey, rejoice!" Worship God for making good on His promises to you! Three annual festivals are mentioned: the Feast of Unleavened Bread (which we have already studied), the Feast of Harvest (also known as Feast of Weeks or Pentecost in the New Testament), and the Feast of Ingathering (also known as Feast of Tabernacles and Feast of Booths).

Feast of Harvest
(Exodus 23:16a; 34:22a)

This harvest celebrated the fruits from the first crops of wheat. It was held seven weeks after the Feast of Unleavened Bread. The people made sacrifices and offerings to the Lord; they ate, worshipped, and rested from their work. God invited everyone to the party (Deuteronomy 16:11). As an act of love, justice, and mercy, He required the harvesters to leave residuals of the crops in the fields so the poor and the aliens could glean from them.

Feast of Ingathering
(Exodus 23:16b)

Clearly, God didn't want His people to become so self-righteous that they didn't know how to have a great time! Rejoicing continued with the Feast of Booths because "the LORD your God will bless you in all your harvest and in all the work of your hands, and your joy will be complete" (Deuteronomy 16:15). The Feast of Ingathering was in celebration to close out the harvest season in the fall beginning on the fifteenth day of the seventh month (Ethanim, around September/October). We might think of this as a fall festival which lasted seven days. It began with a day of rest from work, along with a holy convocation or worship service on the first day. The community feasted from the land's abundant produce and celebrated with singing and dancing. The eighth day was a more somber occasion that included a holy convocation or worship service, and the people rested from their work.

The festivals are designed to honor God's mercy and generosity to the children He loves and provides for. Even in the Old Testament, we have opportunities to sing, "How deep the Father's love for us, how vast beyond all measure."[28]

---

28 Stuart Townend, "How Deep the Father's Love," 1995, Thankyou Music, https://www.stuarttownend
    .co.uk/song/how-deep-the-fathers-love-for-us/.

Help Is on the Way

In addition to providing opportunities for celebration, God promises to send the Israelites help for their journey in the form of an angel. This angel will serve as God's presence, protection, and provision for the Israelites. The angel will guide the Israelites to the promised land where God has already marked out territory (Exodus 23:20, 23, 31). They are to obey God's angel as God's holy representative, and not rebel because the angel has authority both to discipline and fight for them against their enemies (vv. 21–22). This marks the end of the book of the covenant before the Israelites confirm that they will keep covenant with God and not with the false idols that are worshipped in the land where they are going.

Questions

Our lives are sometimes so busy or we feel too self-important that we neglect the opportunities God gives us to rest and celebrate. What occasions do you take to rest or exhaust all of your vacation days?

What are some low-cost celebratory opportunities?

Day 5

Making Covenant with God

SCRIPTURE READING
Exodus 24

Jackie Hill Perry focuses her book *Holier Than Thou* on the premise of God's holiness. "'Holy' means 'to cut' or 'to separate.' When applied to everything outside of God, whatever is holy is whatever is set apart unto and for God. . . . God isn't holy simply because He's alive. . . . God is holy because God has *always* been alive."[29] God is holy because He is self-existent, meaning He is, has always been, and forever will be God all by himself. And God is holy because He is transcendent, meaning that "God is totally unique from everything there is."[30] And "because God is holy, all that He says is true and all that He does is good."[31] This is the essence of how God reveals himself to Israel, and the covenant reflects the holy people they are.

The symbolism in Exodus 24 reveals God's holiness and His might (vv. 15–17). In chapter 19, we read, "There was thunder and lighting, with

---

29 Jackie Hill Perry, *Holier Than Thou: How God's Holiness Helps Us Trust Him* (Nashville: B&H Publishing, 2021), 20–21.
30 Perry, *Holier Than Thou*, 23.
31 Perry, 54.

a thick cloud over the mountain. . . . Mount Sinai was covered with smoke, because the LORD descended on it in fire. The smoke billowed up from it like smoke from a furnace, and the whole mountain trembled violently" (vv. 16, 18). God is near. While selected leaders accompanied Moses up the mountain, the rest of the community remained at the base, and Moses alone entered God's presence.

On the mountain, Moses ratified Israel's covenant with God. Then he gave the instructions to God's people, who responded together, "We will do everything the LORD has said; we will obey" (Exodus 24:7). Moses wrote down the law (v. 4). Then the covenant was confirmed through blood sacrifice, the Lord's presence, and a covenantal meal. Just like the hopeful promises in the new covenant, the Lord sealed this covenant with the shedding of blood. "Moses then took the blood, sprinkled it on the people and said, 'This is the blood of the covenant that the LORD has made with you in accordance with all these words'" (v. 8). Then God gave Moses the stone tablets which included the writings of the Ten Commandments.

Moses engaged young men in the sacrifice preparations. We also notice that the young man Joshua (who led the battle against the Amalekites) is serving as Moses's aide (v. 13). Worshipping God and leading His people is an intergenerational affair. Joshua accompanies Moses up the mountain, as Moses leaves Aaron and Hur in charge of the community. The narrative picks up from this place in chapter 32.

God's Word to God's People

"Hear, O Israel: . . . these commandments that I give you today are to be on your hearts. Impress them on your children. Talk about them when you sit at home and when you walk along the road, when you lie down and when you get up. Tie them as symbols on your hands and bind them on your foreheads. Write them on the doorframes of your houses and on your gates" (Deuteronomy 6:4, 6–9). God wants Israel to remember.

"[He] expected the elderly, the wise, and the spiritually mature to teach their children and their children's children about Yahweh (God)—both who he was and what he had done. . . . Part of the reason that the Israelites persisted in sin is because the people did not remember and the elderly did not teach!"[32]

If Pharaoh had his way, Moses would have been forcefully drowned with the other Hebrew boys of his generation, but Moses made safe passage through the Nile River. As he grew, the elders cried out to God because of their enslavement and God heard the cries of His disinherited people. God was not silent when confronting the injustices of Pharaoh; He raised up a deliverer. God cut through the evil and pride of Egypt with the precision of a samurai blade, then brought them out of darkness to give them a hope and a future. God made them His very own and set them apart as His holy representatives on the earth.

Question

Over the course of your faith journey, what have you learned about God's holiness?

---

32 Natasha Sistrunk Robinson, *Mentor for Life: Finding Purpose through Intentional Discipleship* (Grand Rapids, MI: Zondervan, 2016), 199.

Remembering God's Just Work

SCRIPTURE READING
Deuteronomy 4:1–20

Never forget that this is the just God we serve. He is the one who takes bad situations and makes them right. He takes people who are without a name and gives them names, those who are without a family and provides a home. God takes the outcast and oppressed and gives them voices and responsibility, and raises them up for leadership. He makes them great because their presence, purpose, and prosperity are attached to His own reputation. Working to create a just society helps us to remember who God is, what He has already done, and our desperate need to trust and depend on Him to fulfill His redemptive purpose for all creation. If we avail ourselves, God can continue building His great legacy through us.

> Knowing the pain, history, violence, and silence that have shaped the African American narrative infuses how I read the Scriptures. I come from a marginalized and

oppressed people group that was enslaved for more than three hundred years, so I try to imagine the helplessness and hopelessness that the Hebrew people felt as an entire generation of their boys were thrown into the Nile River. What would be worse: knowing that the actual genocide took place, knowing that people in positions of power in the empire stood by and said nothing, or knowing that nothing would be done about this loss of innocent lives—that justice would not be served? This is a painful narrative that is quite familiar to African Americans. Murder by the state. Silence. Then nothing. The heart dies a slow death. The painful reality of this death emotionally cripples us, and black people have been conditioned to say, "Thank you," and take our lethal doses with a smile.

But I am not without hope. We see from Moses' story that God hears the cries of the oppressed. God enters our pain, through our suffering, even in the silence. If healing is to come, then this pain must be named and confronted. We cannot look away. With every truth-telling moment, we can better discern what these moments reveal about our history, our authentic selves, our leadership journey, and our hope for a better future.

Natasha Sistrunk Robinson, *A Sojourner's Truth*

Group Discussion

1. Time of sharing: From this chapter's exercise, share your summary response to the question, "What makes a just society?" Document and reflect on the responses that you have heard from others in your group.

2. In the work of advocacy and the fight for justice, sometimes the injured parties, rather than the benefactors, are doing the most work. Given our patriarchal society, what responsibilities do men have to create equity for women?

3. What responsibilities do White people have to create a more just society for People of Color?

4. What responsibilities do rich people have to create a more just society for the impoverished? (For context: most of the world's population lives on two dollars or less per day.)[33]

5. What responsibilities do adults have to create a more just society for *all* vulnerable children?

_____

_____

_____

_____

_____

_____

_____

_____

_____

_____

_____

---

33   Andrea Peer, "Global Poverty: Facts, FAQs, and How to Help," World Vision, August 23, 2021, https://www.worldvision.org/sponsorship-news-stories/global-poverty-facts.

Building the Tabernacle and Becoming the Priesthood

Therefore, holy brothers and sisters, who share in the heavenly calling, fix your thoughts on Jesus, whom we acknowledge as our apostle and high priest. He was faithful to the one who appointed him, just as Moses was faithful in all God's house. Jesus has been found worthy of greater honor than Moses, just as the builder of a house has greater honor than the house itself. For every house is built by someone, but God is the builder of everything. "Moses was faithful as a servant in all God's house," bearing witness to what would be spoken by God in the future. But Christ is faithful as the Son over God's house. And we are his house, if indeed we hold firmly to our confidence and the hope in which we glory.

Hebrews 3:1–6

Day 1

Commentary

This week covers a lot of material, so instead of reading most of the Scripture on the first day as we have done in previous weeks, I will encourage you to read Scripture on the appropriate days throughout the week. We will discuss practical leadership lessons, explore our responsibilities to work and exercise spiritual gifts, and highlight the significance and the establishment of the priesthood and the tabernacle. Finally, we will shift our attention and connect Exodus to the tabernacling and priesthood of Jesus, and what that awareness means for New Testament believers.

Leadership Skills for God's Work

SCRIPTURE READING
Exodus 38:21–31; 39:32–43

Moses fades into the background in these chapters, and that is fitting. Once the leadership roles and responsibilities are clear, tasks have been delegated to competent people, and the community is fully engaged and mobilized for the work, the leader's name or presence doesn't have to take center stage. However, we know that Moses is present, on task, and focused on the work at hand. Moses continues to provide instruction and accountability. In Exodus 38:21–31, Moses takes inventory and inspects the supplies. We know that the people gave generously and with willing hearts for God desires to bless us when we make offerings in faith and with pure hearts.[1] However, the people didn't know God's ways. As their leader, it is Moses's responsibility to check the quality of what was offered.

Moses calls for an inspection. "Count the materials, all of it." While I was serving in the military, inspections started with small things like the proper shining of shoes, ironing uniforms, the cleanliness of our bedrooms and work spaces, our physical fitness, and random drug tests. By the time I was commissioned as an officer in the US Marine Corps to handle millions of federal government dollars, the stakes increased significantly. When I was stationed with the deployable unit Second Maintenance Battalion at Camp Lejeune, North Carolina, our inspections included the auditing of weapons, vehicles, financial accounts, and safety protocols, and the review of policies that addressed issues like the proper disposal of hazardous materials. As a leadership lesson, I learned early to "expect what you inspect."

That is what Moses is doing. He is not assuming, just because the people generously offered supplies for the tabernacle, that what they offered was of good quality or that what they offered was needed to accomplish the task. The builders knew when they had enough because Moses established accountability and quality control measures. Once the tabernacle was completed, Moses conducted another inspection (Exodus 39:32–43). Here again, Moses inspects everything. He looks at the clasps, the frames, the posts, and the bases. Moses inspects all the furniture. With this practice, we see another leadership principle at work, "Trust *and* verify."

No competent person likes a boss who micromanages their work, and it is a good practice when leaders trust their peers, managers, employees,

---

1   Reference the widow's offering (Mark 12:41–44 and Luke 21:1–4) and the believers in community (Acts 4:32–37) in contrast to Ananias and Sapphira (Acts 5:1–11) and the rich young man (Matthew 19:16–26 and Mark 10:17–27).

and support staff. However, Moses received the instructions from God and they are *all* new to serving their divine supervisor. Trust is built over time. Therefore, Moses takes intentional action on the front end. Surely there was communication throughout the project, and Moses finished well by providing that same accountability on the back end. "Moses inspected the work and saw that they had done it just as the LORD had commanded. So Moses blessed them" (v. 43).

Moses blessed the people *after* everything was done to God's satisfaction. Sit with that for a moment. Have there been times in your life when you offered God something that you know wasn't your best, but your attitude said, "That's done, now I can move on"? When working on a ministry or a service project, has your flesh ever whispered, "They better be glad that I offered anything at all"? With this project, we get to reflect on how our entire lives are offerings to God, and how God cares about every detail concerning us including what we offer and how we build. Through the building of the tabernacle, the establishment and practice of leadership, and the sacrificial offerings, we are taught to give God our best *every* time.[2] This is a leadership lesson for our ministry, service, or charity work, and we can also take it into our work spaces to inform our practices for professional development, leadership training, people and project management, and team building. We all need accountability for the products that we produce, the services we provide, the teams that we build, and the relationships that we cultivate at work. As God's witnesses, our quality control measures help keep ethics and standards high; they are safeguards to protect us from trouble. Therefore, it is best to implement these tools of accountability at the very beginning, before you start work, a new professional relationship, or a project. If you have neglected this practice of accountability, there is no better time for you and your team to outline and implement new practices than now.

---

2   Also see Genesis 4:3–7 and 2 Samuel 24:24.

Exercise

As we reflect on professional accountability, we acknowledge that self-leadership also requires personal accountability, and maybe a little help from our friends. Pray before you start this project and again once you complete the first draft. Pray about the categories, the intentions (the motivations behind the intentions), and the people who will support you. Pray that the Holy Spirit will guide you through the process. Make a category chart or vision board outlining the areas of your life that are most important to you. This could include finances, health, mental health and wellness, faith, family, work, hobbies, cultivating new skills, or something else. Under each category, list the names and/or post the images of the people that you admire and why. Who are the leaders in the respective fields? (This can be people that you personally know, or some that you don't.) What goals or vision do you have for building in these areas? What intentions (first step) can you set? Who can hold you accountable in each of these areas? Where are your knowledge, skills, and/or relationship gaps? Now that you have something tangible to work with, what is your next step?

Creative Talents for God's Work

SCRIPTURE READING
Exodus 28:3; 31:1–11; 35:25–36:2

The tabernacle needed creative workers and Bezalel and Oholiab were among those representing this community of creatives with their wisdom, understanding, skill, and knowledge of their craft. They were chosen and appointed by God because they were good at their jobs. Being a person of faith is not an excuse for poor job performance; if anything, our faith can motivate us to represent God well in any space where we are privileged to work. We can all become skilled workers if we understand our purpose, are humble to learn, are disciplined in our pursuit, and stick with something long enough to become an expert.

These formerly enslaved Israelites came out of Egypt with trades that God expected them to use. Whether being a craftsperson, construction worker, or architect, this was their moment to shine. This is the first time that the community was given the opportunity to use their creative skills collectively for God's work. Over the years within Western Christendom, we have created so many divisions and hierarchies which operate against God's good will for His people. We humans are masters of division. We created the "sacred and secular" divides surrounding our work. God does not. From the very beginning, Adam was created for the work of tending a garden (Genesis 2:4–8). That work was holy, beautiful, and Adam completed it in the Lord's presence. In working, Adam bore God's image and mirrored the actions of the one who created him. From the beginning, the Lord God worked to create something out of nothing. Bezalel and this community of creatives could do the same. Together, they created something beautiful for God that the world had never seen before. Let's reconsider the thoughts we keep regarding our work, for "the value of our work isn't . . . found at all in the particular thing we do; it's found in the fact that whatever we do, we do it for our King."[3] God chose Bezalel, Oholiab, and the entire crew for this sacred work.

"God has created each of us for a specific purpose, and he has given us each different passions, talents, abilities, and skills to complete the good works he has prepared."[4] On two separate occasions, we are told that Bezalel was filled with the Spirit of God which enabled his work (Exodus 31:3; 35:31). The Holy Spirit always was, and forever will be, God at work in the world.[5] In Exodus 35:34, God's Spirit also equipped Bezalel and

---

3   Sebastian Traeger and Greg Gilbert, *The Gospel at Work: How Working for King Jesus Gives Purpose and Meaning to Our Jobs* (Grand Rapids, MI: Zondervan, 2013), 136.
4   Natasha Sistrunk Robinson, *Mentor for Life: Finding Purpose through Intentional Discipleship* (Grand Rapids, MI: Zondervan, 2016), 216.
5   Old Testament references: Deuteronomy 34:9; Numbers 11:16–17, 25–27; Micah 3:8. For further study: Natasha Sistrunk Robinson, *Hope for Us: Knowing God through the Nicene Creed* (Grand Rapids, MI:

Oholiab to teach others how to work. The New Testament provides several examples about the spiritual gifts that can be at work in us.[6] These lists—though not exhaustive—can include prophecy, serving or encouraging others, philanthropy, leadership, pastoring, evangelizing, healing and helping others, or administration. These skills are generally not realized until we use them. As New Testament believers, "when we utilize our spiritual gifts for the edification of the body of Christ, we are actually honoring and worshipping God. We are also acknowledging our need for community, because none of our spiritual gifts are fully functional in isolation."[7] God wants His people at work and on mission together.

Bezalel is the leader, and Oholiab is his assistant in carrying out this important work. Bezalel is a descendant of Hur.[8] Hur was given the opportunity to support God's work, and he proved himself faithful. His grandson is following in his footsteps serving the Lord just as he did, but in a different way. Such is the case when the Spirit moves across generations. In God's providence, we are also told that Bezalel is from the tribe of Judah, the tribe that will produce God's chosen king, David. This is the tribe from which Jesus's human lineage is traced. So, the tribe of Judah built the tabernacle before becoming the tabernacle of God (Hebrews 7:14).

Bezalel was filled with the Holy Spirit; he was well trained and ready to work. We see that he is an able teacher who prepares others for the tasks at hand. Some people can have all of that working in their favor and still not do the work God has assigned to them, but not Bezalel; he goes to work with laser focus and precision. Throughout the building of the tabernacle chapters (Exodus 36–38), we read, "Then Bezalel made . . . next he made . . . he also made. . . ." Bezalel took his work seriously. Once he completed one task, he got to work on the next assignment. That fortitude

Credo House Publishers, 2017), 27–42 (lessons 4–5). Only available at Amazon.com.
6   Romans 12:4–8; Ephesians 4:7–13; 1 Corinthians 12; and 1 Peter 4:10–11.
7   Robinson, *Mentor for Life*, 218.
8   Hur was one of the leaders who held Moses's arms up during the battle against the Amalekites (Exodus 17:8–13).

takes discipline and commitment. The formerly enslaved were no strangers to hard work. However, we must remind all people in our society—young and older—about the importance of working hard and finishing what you start. For whatever we do, we must do wholeheartedly as unto the Lord (Colossians 3:23).

Are there appropriate times to quit or step away from a particular job, task, project, or relationship? Absolutely! And how we finish can be an invaluable witness to God's people, and to those we lead and work alongside within the marketplace. So, finish with integrity. Communicate clearly. If possible, give people time to adjust to the change that is about to happen. Set healthy boundaries as you transition. Don't burn bridges as you exit. Nurture the relationships that you want to keep. Write thank-you notes. Ask the Lord how to enter your work tasks and ask the Lord how to finish. Lead well as God instructs and finish well as God directs. These are the leadership lessons that Bezalel offers us. "Bezalel, Oholiab and every skilled person to whom the LORD has given skill and ability to know how to carry out all the work of constructing the sanctuary are to do the work just as the LORD has commanded" (Exodus 36:1). And it was so.

Questions

How well do you perform your work tasks?

What skills or talents are lying dormant in you? What might God be asking you to finish?

Day 2

The Royal Priesthood

SCRIPTURE READING
Exodus 28–29; 39

SUPPLEMENTAL READING
Numbers 3; 8:5–26; 18:1–8, 20–32; Deuteronomy 18:1–8

What is the purpose of the tabernacle and the priesthood? To answer that question, we must begin with the end in mind. The tabernacle and the priesthood reaffirm that Yahweh brought the Israelites out of Egypt, and that the Israelites have been uniquely set apart as God's chosen people (Exodus 29:44–46). God established the tabernacle or Tent of Meeting[9] so the Israelites had a place to worship their divine king. God already expressed His desire for intimacy with Israel, then He invited them to His house or royal palace. The priests served as ministers of God's tabernacle.

---

9   "Tabernacle" and "Tent of Meeting" are mostly used interchangeably throughout the second part of Exodus. However, Exodus 33:7 indicates that Moses also had another tent, referred to as a "tent of meeting" that he would pitch outside of the Israelites' camp (community/city) so he could meet with the Lord. It appears that the "tent of meeting" referred to in Exodus 33:7 was much smaller, was used by Moses, was set apart from the community because God is holy and the people were not, and served a temporary purpose until the tabernacle was completed.

The Priesthood

We saw the leadership position of judges established in Exodus 18; now we witness the establishment of the leadership role of the priesthood. Priests are those who mediate between God and His people. Aaron, Miriam, and Moses came from the tribe of Levi, on their mother's and father's sides (2:1). However, only Aaron and his male descendants are "gifted" (Numbers 18:7) with the title and responsibility of the priesthood. All priests are Levites, but not all Levites are priests. Likewise, all priests served as judges, but not all judges were priests (Ezekiel 44:24).

The Levites were holy or set apart for God (Numbers 8:5–15) to assist Aaron, his four sons,[10] and their male descendants in the work of the tabernacle. The Levites served under their supervision, but only Aaron and his sons could touch the holy furniture or perform priestly duties (3:5–10; 8:18–19, 22; 18:1–4). All Levite men between the ages of twenty-five and fifty years served God and the community in this way. Then they were allowed to retire from their official responsibilities (8:23–26).

Priestly Garments and Consecration

The priesthood was a birthright of Aaron's male descendants throughout generations (Exodus 40:15) and they were required to wear special garments which set them apart from the rest of the community (28:2). Their ceremonial attire was like a work uniform, worn exclusively for the purpose of serving in the tabernacle. It was holy and passed down for generations (29:29–30), so it could not be worn in common places (Ezekiel 44:17–19). The attire was skillfully crafted, and beautifully made with the most expensive material (Exodus 28:2–5). The priestly garments consisted of a chest piece (or breast piece), ephod, robe, tunic, turban, and sash (v. 4).[11]

---

10 Nadab, Abihu, Eleazar, and Ithamar (Numbers 3:2).
11 The priests were also required to wear long linen undergarments so they would not expose themselves, incur guilt, and die while they were ministering before the Lord (Exodus 20:26; 28:42–43).

The garments had important symbolism. The ephod (28:6–14; 39:2–7) was worn with the sash and included two onyx stones, each listing six names of the twelve sons (tribes) of Israel in their birth order. Once mounted on the shoulder piece of the ephod, the stones were set in gold and served as a memorial "for the sons of Israel" before the Lord (28:12). The breast piece (28:15–30; 39:8–21) was attached to the ephod. It contained twelve stones, mounted in four rows, also representing the twelve sons (tribes) of Israel. It was connected to the ephod, so "whenever Aaron [entered] the Holy Place, he [would] bear the names of the sons of Israel over his heart on the breastpiece of decision as a continuing memorial before the LORD" (28:29). The breast piece was like the ephod in this way, but it also served a different purpose of decision-making. The breast piece included the Urim and the Thummim which were positioned over Aaron's heart, so he could make decisions when he entered the Holy Place. Apparently, the Urim and Thummim were like dice, confirming either a positive or negative response from God.[12] After the death and resurrection of Jesus, the apostles in the New Testament used this method of discernment to confirm Matthias as Judas's replacement (Acts 1:12–26).

The ephod was also worn with a robe (Exodus 28:31–35; 39:22–26). Aaron wore it when he entered the Holy Place to minister before the Lord. It contained gold bells at the bottom, which made noise as he moved about to enter or exit the Holy Place, and it signaled to the Israelites that he was still alive. The *African Bible Commentary* highlights this significance:

> The bells are thus . . . a reminder to the priest, and to us, that while it is a privilege to serve the Lord, it is also a frightening thing. It cannot be done with a carefree attitude. On a more positive note, the people can participate in prayers with the priest as they hear him move about within the Holy Place.

---

12   Reference Numbers 27:21; 1 Samuel 23:9–12; 28:6; 30:7–8; Ezra 2:63.

His exit will also be a time of great rejoicing as the people will know that their sins have been atoned for.[13]

The turban (28:36–39; 39:30–31) included a frontal medallion or plate with the ingraining seal, "Holy to the Lord." "It will be on Aaron's forehead, and he will bear the guilt involved in the sacred gifts the Israelites consecrate, whatever their gifts may be. It will be on Aaron's forehead continually so that they will be acceptable to the LORD" (28:38). In this way, Aaron is taking upon himself the guilt of the people. By accepting Aaron, God is communicating that He has accepted the people. The tunic and sashes (28:39–40; 39:27–29) added dignity and honor to the priestly garments.

Once the garments were completed, the priests were confirmed in a consecration ceremony that lasted seven days (Exodus 29). The ceremony included a cleansing with water, followed by the anointing of the priests and the adorning of their ceremonial garments. It included a sacrifice of one bull (used as a sin offering), one ram (used as a burnt offering to atone for the people's sin), and another ram as a sacrifice and special offering to the Lord. The blood from the latter was used to sprinkle on Aaron and his sons and their garments for consecration; the ram's meat was also holy as it was offered up to God, and portions of it could only be eaten by Aaron and his sons on the same day (vv. 31–34). We learn a significant lesson from these chapters: whether it's common things like clothes or furniture, sacred things like animal sacrifices, or the miraculous transfiguration of Moses's face (34:29–35), anything that enters the Lord's presence is changed and can become holy.

Question

Why did God establish the tabernacle and priesthood?

---

13   Tokunboh Adeyemo, ed., *Africa Bible Commentary: A One-Volume Commentary Written by 70 African Scholars* (Grand Rapids, MI: Zondervan, 2006), 123.

Day 3

The Tabernacle

SCRIPTURE READING
Exodus 25–27; 30; 36:8–38:31; 40:1–33

SUPPLEMENTAL READING
Deuteronomy 12

The tabernacle was a portable temple (tent) or "dwelling place" for the Spirit of God. It preceded the building of the first temple by Israel's third king, Solomon, in 957 BCE. God's Spirit is not exclusive to the tabernacle or the temple, for the Bible tells us that "the Most High does not live in houses made by human hands" (Acts 7:48). God's Spirit is everywhere, all the time (7:48–49; 17:24). However, God is choosing to make His presence known to Israel in the tabernacle. Therefore, it was established as a place of worship, where Israel prayed and offered sacrifices to God. They also provided "atonement money," a kind of ransom or a temple tax (Exodus 30:11–16), so the priests could operate the tabernacle.[14]

Building the tabernacle was a major undertaking, which required skilled workers, intentional planning, financial management, and logistics, and none of this would have happened without the generosity of the

---

14 Israel was required to take a census, and every male twenty years or older was required to pay the same price, whether rich or poor, of one half shekel as an offering to the Lord. This act of obedience also prevented a plague from coming upon them whenever they were numbered (Exodus 30:12).

people. Many churches have used Exodus 35:20–29 to support church building funds and capital campaigns, and for good reason. We want Scripture to inform our faith practices. However, I want to challenge us to consider the full context of where Israel is, the society God has called them out of, and the community and witness that He is building through them. God is establishing new traditions among His people. More pertinent is the reality that God has already done a "new thing" among them by making them His own. Therefore, *He is inviting them to invest in God's vision of who they are already becoming as a people of faith and justice*, as the leaders and witnesses of His great power in a foreign land. There is no hidden agenda, no air of making Moses's name great, no manipulation of blessings or cursing. God simply says, "This is what I'm going to do, and you have an opportunity to make an investment in it."

Good investments always bear returns. The people give generously and with open hearts,[15] so much in fact that the leaders restrict them from giving more (36:3–7). As the people brought their gold jewelry, fine linens, and spices, we are given proof of the riches they brought from Egypt. They took goods from their old place of oppression and are now investing them into God's building (25:1–7), the future and hope that God promised. We also see the accountability and integrity of the leaders who did not take more from the people than what was needed to accomplish the task God had given them.

Building a Dwelling Place

God is meticulous when providing instructions for the Israelites to build the tabernacle (Exodus 26) and its furniture. He does not waver when saying, "Make this tabernacle and all its furnishings exactly like the pattern I will show you." (25:9; see v. 40) The main reason for this level

---

15   Reference Exodus 25:2; and 35:5–9, 20–24, 29.

of detail is because He doesn't want the Israelites worshipping in the same way that other nations worship their false deities (Deuteronomy 12:31).

Like the priestly garments, the tabernacle was made of the finest products. Visuals appeal to our senses. In our modern society, we have television networks dedicated to showing us how nonexistent houses can become beautifully decorated homes. There are plenty of details in the text, so as you read, pay attention to the royal colors, imagine the intricacy of the embroidery, the sparkle of the jewels, and the wonder of large furniture pieces that are made or overlaid with pure gold. Try to imagine such a beautiful edifice becoming a reality and how excited the people must have been to see, contribute to, and experience the process of building.

The tabernacle was organized into four parts: the outer court and inner court (Exodus 27:9–19; 38:9–20), the Holy Place, and the Most Holy Place. The outer court was the first place of entry where the Gentiles (any non-Jews and uncircumcised people) remained. The Israelites entered the inner court through the east courtyard where the bronze or brazen altar for burnt offerings and the washbasin (bronze or brazen laver) for the priests were located. There was a veil (curtain) that separated God's Holy Place (His earthly sanctuary) from the courtyard. Only the priests were allowed to enter the Holy Place. There was another veil embroidered with cherubim that separated the Most Holy Place from the Holy Place. Only the high priest could enter God's presence in the Most Holy Place, and only once a year on the Day of Atonement to offer a blood sacrifice for his own sins and for the sins of the people (Hebrews 9:7–8).[16]

The tabernacle contained six pieces of furniture: the ark of the covenant, table of showbread, lampstand, altar of burnt offering, alter of incense, and washbasin. Like the priestly garments, the tabernacle's furniture served

---

16   Reference Leviticus 16; 23:26–32.

specific purposes, and the purpose of the furniture determined its placement in the tabernacle. The Most Holy Place contained the ark of the covenant. Once completed, the ark of the covenant (or ark of the testimony; Exodus 25:10–22; 37:1–9) contained the stone tablets on which the Ten Commandments were written (25:16). It also included a jar of manna—a reminder of the constant provision God made for them on their journey (16:33)—and eventually Aaron's budding staff (Numbers 17:1–10), signifying God's selection of Israel's leadership (Hebrews 9:4). The ark was a chest made of acacia wood and gold on the inside and outside. It was designed for carrying, and it had an atonement cover (sometimes referred to as the "mercy seat") on top with a design feature of two golden cherubim (cherubs, angelic beings) with wings.[17] God told Moses, "Above the cover between the two cherubim that are over the ark of the covenant law, I will meet with you and give you all my commands for the Israelites" (Exodus 25:22).

The Holy Place contained the table of showbread, lampstand, and the alter of incense. The table of showbread (25:23–30; 37:10–16) was made with acacia wood and overlaid with pure gold, and it held the gold dishes which always contained the bread of presence (twelve pieces of bread representing the twelve tribes of Israel). The bread was holy, and only eaten by the priests (Leviticus 24:5–9). The priests kept the beautifully designed golden lampstand (candlestick)[18] burning continuously for practical purposes since they shared rotations and worked twenty-four hours per day. The seven lamps also reflected the "light," a biblical metaphor signifying God's presence and guidance. Therefore, the wicker lamps burned as "a lasting ordinance among the Israelites for the generations to come" (Exodus 27:21). The alter of incense (30:1–10; 37:25–29) was for

---

17 Cherubim were seen as guardians of protection (Genesis 3:24). "*Cherubim* were the traditional guardians of protection of holy places in the Ancient Near East. Apart from the two described here, others were woven into the curtains which surrounded the tabernacle and which separated the Holy of Holies from the Holy Place (26:1, 31)." Gordon J. Wenham, J. Alec Motyer, D. A. Carson, and R. T. France, eds., *New Bible Commentary: 21st Century Edition* (Downers Grove, IL: IVP Academic, 2010), 112.

18 Refence Exodus 25:31–40; 26:35; 27:20–21; 37:17–24; Numbers 8:1–4.

burning the customized fragrant oils every morning and evening as Aaron kept the lamps (30:34–38). A special oil was customized for the purpose of anointing the altar and the other tabernacle furniture (vv. 22–33), making all of it holy unto the Lord.

The inner court contained the altar of burnt offering and the washbasin. These furniture pieces were made with bronze. All the furniture pieces in the Holy and Most Holy Places were made of gold, and as the territory of the tabernacle expanded out toward the community, more common and less costly materials like bronze were used to design the furniture. The meat for sacrifices was cut on the altar of burnt offering (27:1–8; 38:1–7). It was holy unto the Lord as sacrificial offerings were made daily (29:38–43). Making sacrifices was a bloody affair which sealed God's covenant with His people (24:8; Hebrews 9:16–22). Therefore, priests used the bronze washbasin (Exodus 30:17–21; 38:8) or sink to wash their hands and feet prior to entering the Tent of Meeting, and whenever they approached the Lord.

This may not be the most exciting commentary or scriptural reading, but I hope that the specificity helps readers appreciate the degree to which God went to communicate His intentions to the Israelites. Building the tabernacle and preparing the priests for worship were massive undertakings. And they also offer practical lessons for us today:

1. The people invested and engaged in God's work with great excitement, and they continued together until completion.
2. Even when working on such an important project, God told them to keep their spiritual rhythms, including the Sabbath day of rest (31:12–17; 35:1–3). The importance of the work, the scope of the project, or the pressing deadlines are *not* excuses to neglect the Sabbath. Keeping the Sabbath is a humble reminder that we are not God, and God is still at work even when we are not. It also reminds us and our

children that it is God, not our work, which makes us holy (31:13). Resting gives us another opportunity to trust the Lord to deliver the results for our labor.

The tabernacle was set up on the first day of the first month of the second year of their exodus (40:1–2). Aaron and his sons got dressed and prepared to assume their positions as priests (vv. 12–15). The Bible records that "Moses did everything just as the LORD commanded him" (v. 16).[19] He accomplished the mission on time to begin the cycle of annual festivals, and under budget. Moses completed the tabernacle with perfection for it was an image of the divine that was to come (Hebrews 8:3–6; 9:24). By the end of Exodus, we are told that "Moses finished the work" (40:33).

Question

How did studying the tabernacle and the priesthood shape your view of God?

---

19   Reference Exodus 40:19, 21, 23, 25, 29, and 32.

Jesus: The Tabernacling of God

SCRIPTURE READING
Hebrews 3; 4:14–5:10; 8; 9

The establishment of the tabernacle and priesthood in the Old Testament is a foreshadowing of Jesus as the tabernacle and High Priest of the new covenant, a relationship that God offers to Jews *and* Gentiles. That's why the writer of Hebrews encourages us to fix our thoughts upon Jesus who is worthy of greater honor than Moses (3:1–6). The writer informs our theological understanding:

> The law is only a shadow of the good things that are coming—not the realities themselves. For this reason it can never, by the same sacrifices repeated endlessly year after year, make perfect those who draw near to worship. . . . But those sacrifices are an annual reminder of sins. It is impossible for the blood of bulls and goats to take away sins. (10:1, 3–4)

By becoming the sacrifice, tabernacle, and High Priest, Jesus did what was impossible for the old covenant to accomplish because of the sinfulness of the priests and the people. This statement alone demands that we ask the questions: *Who is Jesus? What was His work?* I cannot do full justice to answering questions about the historical Jesus and His significance within the prophetic context of Israel's story. However, I will make a humble attempt to give an overview based on what we have studied in Exodus.

Who Is Jesus?

The Ten Commandments stated that the Israelites were to worship one God. This reflects the monotheism of Judaism and Christianity. According to church history, orthodox Christians believe that God is presented to us in three "persons": the Father, the Son, and the Holy Spirit. "The doctrine of the Trinity is central to biblical Christianity; it describes the relationships among the three members of the Godhead in a manner consistent with the Scriptures. . . . It focuses on who God is, and particularly on the deity of Jesus Christ."[20] On May 20, 325, the first ecumenical council, the Council of Nicaea (Nicaea I), convened to debate the fundamental question: *Is Jesus God?* The council took care to emphasize the word *homoousios*, "a word that expressed that the Father [God] and the Son [God] shared the same essence or being. . . . At this time, a Christian theologian named Athanasius argued that only God can save human beings from sin. . . . Therefore, if Jesus is not God, then Jesus cannot save us."[21] For more on this Trinitarian teaching, consider my Bible study, *Hope for Us: Knowing God through the Nicene Creed.*[22]

The Bible and the Nicene Creed confirm that Jesus is fully God and fully human. While this is a great mystery to us, it does answer our question. At His birth, Jesus was called Immanuel, the very presence of "God with us"

---

20   H. Wayne House, *Charts of Christian Theology and Doctrine* (Grand Rapids, MI: Zondervan, 1992), 43, 48.
21   Natasha Sistrunk Robinson, *Hope for Us: Knowing God through the Nicene Creed* (Grand Rapids, MI: Credo House Publishers, 2017), vii.
22   This resource is only available at Amazon.com.

(Isaiah 7:14; Matthew 1:23). When the Jews asked Jesus to give an account of himself in John's gospel, Jesus replied, "Very truly I tell you . . . before Abraham was born, *I am*" (8:58, emphasis added). As a result, the Jews picked up stones to kill him (v. 59). They responded this way because they understood two things: (1) they knew Moses's story, and (2) they recalled how God introduced himself to Moses at the burning bush (Exodus 3:2, 4, 14). They also knew the law, specifically the seriousness of idol worship and the sin of blasphemy. Jesus claimed divinity, His hearers understood His claim, and as Jews who honored the old covenant, they responded appropriately *if* Jesus were *not* God. However, Jesus continues to use this "I Am" language throughout John's gospel, reaffirming His claim, confirming His work and the purpose of His human existence.

Jesus's Sacrificial Work

Globally, people of different faiths and traditions believe that Jesus was a moral leader, and perhaps a prophet. This is true. However, the Bible reveals that Jesus's life and teaching matter because they place Jesus at a particular point in history for a specific purpose of God. Jesus was born to die. That statement seems simple enough, for we know that humans are mortal creatures, and we will all die eventually. But Jesus is not *only* human; He is also God. His baptism affirmed the oneness of the Trinity (Matthew 3:13–17), as His Father expressed pleasure with His Son because God the Father knew that the Son of God, Jesus, was going to finish His work! Even in His prayers, Jesus, the Son of God, revealed that He existed in unity with God the Father before the world began and He was sent by God the Father to die.[23] Therefore, His death must have significant meaning. As He goes about living as a human and teaching His followers, He shows them that His sole purpose in life is to do the will of His Father.[24]

---

23 Matthew 26:36–45; Mark 14:32–36; Luke 22:42–44; John 17:5, 8, 20–21, 24–25.
24 Matthew 26:36–45; Mark 14:32–36; Luke 2:41–52; 22:42–44; John 4:31–34; 5:30; 6:38–40; 17:1–4; Hebrews 10:7, 9.

For Jesus understood His mission when stating: "For my Father's will is that everyone who looks to the Son and believes in him shall have eternal life, and I will raise them up at the last day" (John 6:40). To accomplish the Father's will, Jesus had to die as a perfect sacrificial offering for all sin (Isaiah 52:13–53:12).

Jesus understood His life's mission. Herein lies the theological and historical proposal Dr. N. T. Wright wrote in the classic work *Jesus and the Victory of God*:

> Jesus took his own story seriously—so seriously that, having recommended to his followers a particular way of being Israel-for-the-sake-of-the-world, he made that way thematic for his own sense of vocation, his own belief about how the kingdom would come through his own work. . . . He would take up the cross. He would be the light of the world. . . . He would be Israel for the sake of the world. He would be the means of the kingdom's coming, both in that he would embody in himself the renewed Israel and in that he would defeat evil once and for all. . . . He would defeat evil by letting it do its worst to him.[25]

In taking His earthly assignment seriously, Jesus becomes the tabernacle and the atoning sacrifice of God for the sake of all humans.

Jesus Is the Perfect Sacrifice

The apostle John wrote about Jesus as "the atoning sacrifice for our sins, and not only for ours but also for the sins of the whole world" (1 John 2:2; see John 3:16). In reference to this verse, Dr. Donald Fairbairn wrote:

---

25 N. T. Wright, *Jesus and the Victory of God*, Christian Origins and the Question of God 2 (Minneapolis, MN: Fortress Press, 1996), 564–65.

The word that the NIV translates "atoning sacrifice" (*hilasmos*) is one of the most important words in the Bible. . . . In general, an atoning sacrifice . . . is something that is offered to God in place of people who are guilty of sin. The idea is that the sin of the guilty people is transferred somehow to this sacrifice, and the sacrifice (usually an animal) is killed in place of the people who deserve to die. God's wrath toward the people's sin is poured out on the sin-bearing sacrifice, which dies under that wrath in place of the guilty people. The idea of the atoning sacrifice is enshrined prominently in the central ceremonies of the Old Testament law.[26]

We have learned that "the law requires that nearly everything be cleansed with blood, and without the shedding of blood there is no forgiveness" (Hebrews 9:22). However, the sacrifices of the old covenant only *symbolized* the removal of sin.[27] We know this because the sacrifices were repeated year after year, and because the people's hearts remained unchanged.

For the sacrifices of old "were not able to clear the conscience of the worshiper. They are only a matter of food and drink and various ceremonial washings—external regulations applying until the time of the new order" (vv. 9–10). Jesus is the new order! Do you see what is happening here? What God the Father has done through His Son, Jesus Christ, is transfer the sins of guilty people (that's all of us) onto the perfect sacrifice that *does* remove the guilt of sin from humans. Jesus's blood makes all the difference. In offering himself as the perfect sacrifice through His death on the cross, Jesus is atoning for the sins of the world, and cleansing those who believe in Him from the inside out (John 3:16).

---

26 Donald Fairbairn, *Life in the Trinity: An Introduction to Theology with the Help of the Church Fathers* (Downers Grove, IL: IVP Academic, 2009), 160. Also see this writing on the significance of Jesus's death on pages 160–83.

27 Fairbairn, *Life in the Trinity*, 160.

Read Hebrews 9:12–15 and 24–28 to see how the writer presents Jesus's sacrifice. Therefore, from Scripture and church history, we honor Jesus Christ as the fulfillment of God's covenant, the perfect sacrificial "Lamb of God, who takes away the sin of the world" (John 1:29).[28]

Question

How does Jesus's offering of himself compare to the sacrificial offerings made in the tabernacle in Exodus?

---

28   Also see 1 Peter 1:18–19.

The Eternal and the New Exodus

SCRIPTURE READING
Hebrews 7

Not only is Jesus the perfect sacrifice, through His death on the cross, but Jesus himself was appointed by God the Father as our eternal high priest (Hebrews 5:5–6), and He has given us the deposit of the Holy Spirit which forever sustains our new covenant with God (Ephesians 1:13–14; 2 Corinthians 1:22).

Jesus Is the Eternal High Priest

In the moment of His excruciating death, "the curtain of the temple was torn in two from top to bottom. The earth shook, the rocks split and the tombs broke open. The bodies of many holy people who had died were raised to life. They came out of the tombs after Jesus' resurrection and went into the holy city and appeared to many people" (Matthew 27:51–53). The new order has arrived![29] Jesus himself is the High Priest, who has torn down the veil granting all those who believe *full access* into the Most

---

29   Hebrews 8; 9:11; and 10:9.

Holy Place. Dr. James Montgomery Boice wrote, "Nothing could be more human than Jesus' death by crucifixion. Nothing could be more divine than the darkening of the sky, the tearing of the veil of the temple, the opening of the graves of the saints buried near Jerusalem, and the triumphant rending of the tomb on that first Easter morning."[30] Jesus got up! His death is as sure as His resurrection!

The resurrection is the good news! Boice summarizes the centrality of the cross this way:

> The good news is not just that God became man, nor that God has spoken to reveal a proper way of life to us, or even that death, the great enemy, is conquered. Rather, the good news is that sin has been dealt with (of which the resurrection is proof); that Jesus has suffered its penalty for us as our representative, so that we might never have to suffer it; and that therefore all who believe in him can look forward to heaven.[31]

The cross proves that Jesus alone is our great High Priest! "I am the way and the truth and the life," He says. "No one comes to the Father except through me" (John 14:6). Jesus has become the *sole* mediator between God and humans (1 Timothy 2:5). No pastor, spiritual leader, spouse, or government official can fill that role for us. If anyone tells you otherwise, they are looking to usurp the authority of God in your life. They are lying, and not telling the truth. Why would anyone accept a superficial substitute when the perfect and eternal has been made available to them? Jesus is God's guarantee of a better covenant where we can have an intimate relationship with God and receive His assurance that He will not change His mind concerning this (Hebrews 7:17–22)! "Because Jesus lives forever, he has a permanent

---

30 James Montgomery Boice, *Foundations of the Christian Faith: A Comprehensive and Readable Theology* (Downers Grove, IL: InterVarsity Press, 1989), 279.
31 Boice, *Foundations of the Christian Faith*, 291–92.

priesthood. Therefore he is able to save completely those who come to God through him, because he always lives to intercede for them" (vv. 24–25).

Who is the perfect blood sacrifice that forever cleanses and washes away the sins of the world (10:14)? Jesus. Who is the eternal High Priest? Jesus. Who stays in service to do His Father's will, intercedes, and keeps watch over us all day and all night long? Jesus. Who keeps the lamps burning on the lampstand because He has offered himself as the "light of the world" and "the light of life" (John 8:12)? Jesus. Who doesn't have to wait for manna to fall out of the sky, or bake bread every day to sit on a table in the Holy Place, because He is the "bread of life" (6:35)? Jesus. Who doesn't need another witness, because He is a witness and testimony unto himself (8:13–19; Hebrews 6:13–18)? Jesus! It's Jesus. Always Jesus. Only Jesus.

Not only is Jesus's priesthood perfect; it is also permanent![32] Read Hebrews 7:23–28. Thanks be to God, "we have this hope as an anchor for the soul, firm and secure" (6:19). Finally, because of God's grace and mercy, and Jesus's humanity, we need not fear when we approach our great High Priest. "For we do not have a high priest who is unable to empathize with our weaknesses, but we have one who has been tempted in every way, just as we are—yet he did not sin. Let us then approach God's throne of grace with confidence, so that we may receive mercy and find grace to help us in our time of need" (4:15–16). Jesus sympathizes with us in our weaknesses and in our temptation because He understands the human experience.[33] Therefore, we are encouraged to approach Jesus in the Most Holy Place, in the most holy way of our humility to ask Him for help in our time of need. His throne is not a throne of fear, but one of grace. Grace means that God consistently gives us good things—like himself, the perfect sacrificial lamb—that we don't

---

32   Psalm 110:4; Hebrews 5:6; 6:20; 7:17–19, 21; 9:12.

33   For reference regarding one of Jesus's temptations, see Matthew 4:1–11. I believe that Jesus was also tempted to forgo the cross as He prayed fervently in the garden of Gethsemane, and that He was praying to withstand the temptations of the enemy every time He drew away to a quiet place to pray.

deserve. In addition to grace, we also receive mercy. Mercy is when God withholds bad things—like death—which we do deserve because of our sin. Jesus, the High Priest, is always on the job to help in any time of trouble (Psalm 46:1).

Tabernacles and the New Exodus

Because Jesus is the tabernacling of God, our mediator, and great High Priest, we are now partakers of the new exodus. Dr. N. T. Wright wrote: "As a matter of history . . . Jesus of Nazareth was conscious of a vocation . . . given him by the one he knew as 'father,' to enact in himself what, in Israel's scriptures, God has promised to accomplish all by himself. He would be the pillar of cloud and fire for the people of the new exodus. He would embody in himself the returning and redeeming action of the covenant God."[34] We have already explored our rights and responsibilities as the priesthood of all believers, and to that we can add another metaphor. Because of the incarnation of Jesus, we get to collectively become a living tabernacle. It is no longer the seven lamps on the lampstand that must always remain burning. "You are the light of the world" (Matthew 5:14), so shine continuously as a witness through your good deeds and worship of the Father (v. 16).

In response to Wright's presentation of the historical Jesus, and what that means for the ethics of God's new covenant people, Dr. Richard B. Hays wrote:

1. Jesus clearly understood himself to be calling and forming a community.
2. This community was a new covenant community, and it was therefore to be characterized by the renewed heart, a changed heart.

---

34 N. T. Wright, *Jesus and the Victory of God*, Christian Origins and the Question of God 2 (Minneapolis, MN: Fortress Press, 1996), 653.

3. This new-covenant people was not to make common cause with the resistance movement. Instead, they are called to the way of creative nonviolent resistance.

4. These followers were called to live by the jubilee principle among themselves.

5. This community was to be a light to the world.[35]

"Wright pictures Jesus as a man of action, the organizer of a movement. [Jesus] was seeking to give his followers a new vision of their identity that would transform their behavior."[36] If we conclude that Jesus is calling us to a "do better" life, then we are sorely mistaken. We are just as fallible as the Israelites and the priests who represented them. That's where the work of the third person of the Trinity, the Holy Spirit, kicks in.

The Holy Spirit testifies that the new covenant is *not* kept through rituals or sacrifices in a physical tabernacle, or the laws that are written on stones. The Holy Spirit is alive and at work in us to make us holy. The Spirit testifies that the law is now written on the hearts and minds of those who believe, and that God will completely remove the sins from the believers and remember them no more.[37] Because Christ is the tabernacle, we have become the tabernacle of God because God's Spirit is dwelling within those who hold firmly to the hope of Christ's faithful sacrifice (Hebrews 3:6). The Holy Spirit is our internal deposit that we are completely forgiven in Christ (10:18). This is our blessed hope: because of who Jesus is and the work of the Holy Spirit in us, we—the believers and beneficiaries of the new covenant—have become a royal priesthood, heirs to God's throne, a holy nation, a community that belongs to God, a justice movement, the tabernacle of God, and people who are on the journey to freedom through a new exodus. This is God's promise to us! Therefore, "let us draw near to

---

35 Richard B. Hays, "Victory over Violence: The Significance of N. T. Wright's Jesus for New Testament Ethics," in *Jesus and the Restoration of Israel: A Critical Assessment of N. T. Wright's Jesus and the Victory of God*, ed. Carey C. Newman (Downers Grove, IL: IVP Academic, 1999), 146–47.

36 Hays, "Victory over Violence," 147.

37 Jeremiah 31:31–34; Hebrews 8:10; 10:14–17.

God with a sincere heart and with the full assurance that faith brings. . . . Let us hold unswervingly to the hope we profess, for he who promised is faithful. And let us consider how we may spur one another on toward love and good deeds" (vv. 22–24).

Question

Jesus makes a new exodus possible for those who believe in Him. When we are no longer enslaved by the kingdoms of this world, we can become citizens of God's kingdom. What hope do you have in the person and work of Jesus Christ?

An Invitation from Jesus

SCRIPTURE READING
Psalm 23

We are nearing the end of our Exodus Bible study, but it is only the beginning of the long wilderness journey that Moses will take with the Israelites. The wilderness journey is not uncommon for God's people. When Christians ask me, "What is the most important lesson that you have learned?" I sometimes reply, "Let the wilderness do its work." The wilderness is an able teacher; it informs our beliefs about God, ourselves, and others. Journeying through the wilderness is both challenging and humbling. *If* we want to come out on the other side of our wilderness journey alive and free, *then* we need to turn our attention toward the humble and suffering servant, Jesus. Jesus knows the way.

Whether you are parenting a teenager, correcting a college student, running an organization, or mentoring a friend, the opportunity to journey through the wilderness is a sacred invitation from God. Even Jesus was led by the Holy Spirit to take this journey before beginning his earthly ministry (Matthew 4:1–11). The wilderness brings us to the humble path. It reminds us of the great charge to take up our cross and follow Jesus (Mark 8:34). . . .

There is nothing glamorous about the teachings of the wilderness. In solitude and isolation, we learn how to do the internal work, how to surrender to God. And he teaches us how to lead ourselves so we can effectively lead others on the sacred way. . . . If we respond in obedience to his invitation, we may experience the miraculous goodness and grace of his transformation in our own lives. . . .

Our responsibility on the humble path is to tend to our assigned work, understanding that being a servant in God's kingdom is the first priority. The second priority is extending this invitation to other broken people on the path.

Natasha Sistrunk Robinson, *A Sojourner's Truth*

Group Discussion

1. How does the old covenant lay a foundation for the new covenant?

2. How has this study in Exodus informed your faith as the tabernacle and priesthood of God?

3. Where have you experienced wilderness moments in your life, and what have those experiences taught you about God, yourself, and other humans?

4. Time of sharing: How might your group support your exercise from this week?

5. What leadership lessons have you learned or what life skills have been reinforced through observing Moses, Bezalel, and the Israelite community at work together?

_____

_____

_____

_____

_____

_____

_____

_____

_____

_____

_____

_____

_____

_____

_____

_____

_____

_____

_____

_____

_____

_____

_____

Beginning the Journey to Freedom

---

*The Word became flesh and made his dwelling among us.
We have seen his glory, the glory of the one and only Son,
who came from the Father, full of grace and truth. . . .
Out of his fullness we have all received grace in place
of grace already given. For the law was given through
Moses; grace and truth came through Jesus Christ.
No one has ever seen God, but the one and only Son,
who is himself God and is in closest relationship
with the Father, has made him known.*

John 1:14, 16–18

Day 1

Commentary

SCRIPTURE READING
Exodus 32–34; 40:34–38

We pick up the narrative from Exodus 24 in chapter 32 where Israel worshipped a golden calf. Not long before, they confessed, "Everything the LORD has said we will do" (Exodus 24:3). Now, they are violating the law in the most grievous way by breaking the greatest commandment. They make an idol for themselves to worship, and they give that idol credit for bringing them out of Egypt. In doing so, they also break the first and second commandments, ignoring the truth, "I am . . . God, who brought you out of Egypt, out of the land of slavery" (20:2). They worshipped a created thing rather than the Creator, and we see in them clearly that "anybody who has ever praised an idol for its love was actually giving their 'thank you' away to the wrong person."[1] (See Romans 1:21.) As a result, thousands of Israelites lose their lives.

Moses does his best to remain faithful, but he is weary now and angry with the people. They should have known better. His brother, Aaron—who was destined to become Israel's high priest—neglected his leadership so the people cast off all restraint. The Israelites persisted in their will to

---

1   Jackie Hill Perry, *Holier Than Thou: How God's Holiness Helps Us Trust Him* (Nashville: B&H Publishing, 2021), 97.

sin, so Aaron let them. He also participated in the darkness. The darkness is dangerous; death is coming quickly, so Moses must act fast. The righteous shed the blood of the guilty parties. Moses seeks to make atonement for the people's sin with prayer and petition, and eventually by offering up his own life on their behalf. In this, he models the way of Jesus. Most times when we are in dangerous and dark situations, it is best to humbly enter God's presence through prayer. God is holy, the people are not, so God seeks to change course. He is not abandoning the Israelites; they have abandoned Him, and by sending them on their way God is seeking to preserve their lives.

Moses isn't having it. While the Israelites are no longer enslaved physically, their mental and spiritual enslavement is a reality. They don't believe that freedom is within their reach, but Moses can sense it in his spirit. Moses believes God, so in Exodus 15:13–17, he has a freedom song on his lips. Moses knows that the freedom that he sung about will not come to fruition without God, so he waits for the assurance that God will accompany the people for the remainder of their exodus journey. Moses's leadership posture is simple: either God goes with the people or the people will not go. What other guarantee will they have of success? God graced Moses with the clarity of humility, vulnerability, knowledge, and understanding.

Moses fasts again for forty days and forty nights. The glory of the Lord comes, and God's guidance prevails. At the conclusion of the book, the Lord is present with His people.

Questions

Where are you on your exodus journey?

What assurance do you have that God is with you?

Day 2

Idolatry Leads to Death

SCRIPTURE READING
Exodus 32:1–29

In chapter 32, Moses is up the mountain to receive the covenant commandments from God. He left Aaron and Hur in charge (Exodus 24:14). It doesn't take long—a little more than a month—for the people to forget everything that God taught them and revert to the ways of Egypt. They asked Aaron to make them a god (or gods) to worship because they don't know what happened to Moses (32:1). Perhaps they assumed that Moses was dead, but even if he was, Yahweh is not! In their impatience, they craft a plan.

This is a warning about the package that impatience can deliver to you. Inspired by his book *Urban Apologetics: Restoring Black Dignity with the Gospel*, pastor and editor Dr. Eric Mason did an Instagram post about witchcraft and Christianity.[2] In the video, he presents witchcraft as a shortcut into the spiritual domain. In other words, there is danger when people try to get power in the supernatural without accessing it in God's way. He said that people get impatient because God's process is to sanctify us before He can trust us with supernatural things. When we have

---

2   Eric Mason, "Witchcraft and Christianity," Instagram, August 11, 2021, https://www.instagram.com/tv/CSc4lwABuGX/.

been conditioned to covet everything, it is easy to turn our petitions into demands. "God, give me what I want now!" When we respond this way, we have become gods unto ourselves and are in grave danger.

Israel makes a demand of Aaron, "Come, make us gods who will go before us" (32:1). Aaron does not resist; he doesn't remind them of God's instruction; he doesn't redirect or correct; he doesn't even wash his hands of the situation (see Matthew 27:24). He joins right in, asking the people to bring him their gold and jewelry. Aaron melted the gold down and shaped it into an image of a golden calf (Exodus 32:2–4). Then they said, "These are your gods, Israel, who brought you up out of Egypt" (v. 4). They worship the idol, giving it credit for what God has done. But Aaron doesn't stop there. He builds an altar for the created thing and calls for a "festival to the LORD" (v. 5). On the next day, the people rise to offer up sacrifices to the created thing, and "afterward they sat down to eat and drink and got up to indulge in revelry" (v. 6). This is syncretism, an "attempt to assimilate differing or opposite doctrines and practices, especially between philosophical and religious systems, resulting in a new system altogether in which the fundamental structure and tenets of each have been changed."[3] When God says that He is jealous (34:14), He is saying: God. Will. Not. Share. Worship. With. An. Idol. Period.

Moses is on the mountain minding his business and focusing on what God told him to do. Then God says to him, "Go get your people!" God mentions how quickly the people have turned away, how stubborn and rebellious they are (32:7–9). God is so angry; He doesn't know what to do. God is not like an indecisive human. He is conflicted because according to God's own law, the right thing to do is to kill them all, which He considers. He says to Moses, "Leave me alone so that my anger may burn against them and that I may destroy them. Then I will make you into a great nation." (v. 10)

---

3   Stanley J. Grenz, David Guretzki, and Cherith Fee Nordling, *Pocket Dictionary of Theological Terms* (Downers Grove, IL: InterVarsity Press, 1999), 111.

God makes Moses an offer that he can't refuse, but Moses doesn't take Him up on it. Moses has the heart of a servant leader. Instead of seeking self-gratification, Moses starts to wing it. He questions God, "What will the Egyptians think about this?" He pleads with God to repent. Moses reminds God of Israel's history and the promises that God made to their ancestors. Although Moses is on the horns of a dilemma and is improvising, he is not doing so without context. Moses is following the example of Abraham, making bold requests, negotiating with God (Genesis 18:16–33). He is doing so while understanding God's heart and using God's own words (Exodus 32:11–13). Because the Spirit at work in Moses resonates with God's own Spirit, God changes course concerning the people (v. 14).

Seeing is believing. Moses and his mentee, Joshua, went down the mountain with the two stone tablets as the noise from Israel's camp increased in their ears. Joshua thought they were at war (v. 17), but the truth was far worse. Upon their arrival at camp, Moses saw the calf and the dancing, and he became so angry that he threw the tablets down and they broke at his feet (v. 19). He takes immediate action to destroy the calf, calls for its burning; they ground what is left into powder. He threw the powder in water and forced the people to drink it (v. 20). This is polluted water! It's as if Moses is using the very thing that we all need to live and sustain our physical bodies as humans (i.e., water) to enact the reality of drinking the spiritual death and destruction they have brought upon themselves.

Idols Demand an Account

Immediately, Moses goes to Aaron to ask, "What did these people do to you, that you led them into such great sin?" (v. 21). Let's not be so quick to judge Aaron, because we are all prone to sin in the same way when it feels convenient. Need biblical proof beyond your personal testimony? Paul took the same posture as Moses when he asked the churches in Galatia questions regarding their disregard for Jesus Christ: "You foolish Galatians! Who has bewitched you? Before your very eyes Jesus Christ was clearly portrayed as crucified. . . . Are you so foolish? After beginning by means of the Spirit, are you now trying to finish by means of the flesh?" (Galatians 3:1, 3). Aaron has a chance to confess his sin, repent, drop to his knees, wail, mourn, and beg for God's forgiveness. Aaron does none of it. Instead, he responds like a little child.

Reading this conversation is like remembering when you asked your daughter if she broke something, and she looks you straight in the eyes with her cute face and lies with confidence. "I don't know how it got broken. It just happened." And sometimes, if the kid has other siblings and they are not around to defend themselves, the child who is under scrutiny will pass on the blame. "He did it." That's how Aaron responds to Moses. He makes excuses and blames the people. There is nothing new here, folks (Genesis 3:11–13). As if believing his own lie, Aaron said with confidence that he put the gold in a furnace, and he doesn't know how the calf got there (Exodus 32:22–24). By neglecting his leadership, Aaron has made a mockery of the people and embarrassed God in front of their enemies (v. 25).

In this instance, Aaron exercises poor leadership. I learned early as a second lieutenant in the US Marine Corps that if things go well with my unit, always give the people under my command credit for the success. However, if we fail, then I must take full responsibility as the leader. Community and team failures are always the result of poor leadership. Aaron doesn't take ownership for his actions or the fact that the people are "running wild" under his care. We know that Aaron will become Israel's first high priest, representing the people before God. However, just like the first Adam (Genesis 3) who represented all humanity before God, Aaron fails at his charge. This is the unfortunate reality of living in a fallen world. No matter people's good intentions, at some point humans fail us. That's why we must put our hope and trust in the unfailing God! Jesus is the second High Priest and the second Adam[4] who perfectly represents us before the Father and keeps our covenant with God. Jesus takes ownership of His responsibility, and He cannot fail!

God's Wrath Leads to Judgment

"Moses saw that the people were running wild and that Aaron had let them get out of control and so become a laughingstock to their enemies. So he stood at the entrance to the camp and said, 'Whoever is for the Lord, come to me.' And all the Levites rallied to him" (Exodus 32:25–26). Moses told the Levites to strap a sword to their side and go throughout the camp killing anyone that enticed the people to worship the golden calf. The "kill order" goes out because "without the shedding of blood there is no forgiveness" (Hebrews 9:22). According to the law, blood sacrifices were offered up for unintentional sins, or sins for which people were not aware. We don't always know when we are being prideful, ungrateful, selfish, jealous, slothful, or covetous. Therefore, God's grace covers the multitude of these sins as symbolized by the Old Testament's ritual sacrifices. However, there are no sacrifices made for the sins of commission, the willful acts of disobedience. According to the Old Testament law, the penalty for sins of commission, particularly when other humans have been physically harmed, is often death. Referencing the Old Testament law, the writer of Hebrews shares, "If we deliberately keep on sinning after we have received the knowledge of the truth, no sacrifice for sins is left, but only a fearful expectation of judgment and of raging fire that will consume the enemies of God" (10:26–27). That dreadful day has come for the Israelites. Three thousand of them die (Exodus 32:28).

Sometimes believers are way too comfortable with sin; we all have idols that need burning. If we are honest, sometimes we hold on to idols because death doesn't seem imminent or as serious as this passage presents.

---

4   Reference Romans 5:12–21 and 1 Corinthians 15:22, 45–49.

However, when the Bible reads that "the consequence of sin is death, [it] implies both physical separation of the soul from the body [as reflected in this passage] and, more significantly, alienation from God."[5] Unlike Aaron and the Israelites, Moses has been in God's presence long enough to know that living apart from God is no life at all.

Sin is the cause of our physical death, and it can result in alienation from God. Idolatry leads to the grave. That's the truth. And, as the blood of their sinful neighbors dripped from their swords, the Levites were blessed for their obedience (Exodus 32:29). These men chose God above all else and were set apart as a result.

Question

What idol(s) might you offer up to Jesus?

---

5 Donald Fairbairn, *Life in the Trinity: An Introduction to Theology with the Help of the Church Fathers* (Downers Grove, IL: IVP Academic, 2009), 167.

Day 3

Submitted and Humble Leadership

SCRIPTURE READING
Exodus 32:30–33:11; 34:10–35

My guess is that no one within Israel's camp slept well that night. The next day, Moses got up and went back up the mountain to make atonement for the people. He confessed the people's sin of idolatry and asked for God's forgiveness (Exodus 32:31–32). Then Moses does something unexpected. He offers himself as a replacement for the people. He said to God, "Please forgive their sin—but if not, then blot me out of the book you have written" (v. 32).[6] Moses is willing to give up his eternal inheritance. "My life for theirs" is his offering to God, and with this statement, he models the way of Jesus Christ. God says, "No, sir, everyone must give an account for their own life and their own sin."

When God sends Moses back to lead the people, He does so with a warning: "Judgment is still coming." While Moses attempted to make restitution with the Levites (vv. 25–29), God's justice was not yet satisfied.

---

6 The Book of Life is a book which lists the names of those who have been appointed unto salvation to spend eternity with God: Psalm 69:28; Daniel 12:1; Luke 10:20; Philippians 4:3; and Revelation 3:5; 13:8; 17:8; 20:12–15.

This is a troubling thought particularly in our "world [that] presents God as . . . [if we] expect Him to forgive without justice or be merciful without condemnation [because we] want a God who is so indifferent toward His glory that He would lay aside His righteousness (if possible) so that He could declare [us] innocent. . . . [But] if God is holy, God must be just."[7] God is merciful and Jesus is on the way, but for now, God says, "When the time comes for me to punish, I will punish them for their sin" (v. 34). Because of their idolatry, God initiates a plague which causes the death of many others (v. 35). God knew what Moses could not know. He saw the darkened hearts of those remaining, and so God was still cleaning up camp.

God tells Moses to get back to work, preparing the people to enter the land of promise. God promises to send an angel to accompany them, but God himself has no intention of continuing the journey (33:1–3). God promises to uphold His end of the covenant: Israel will get there, the land will be plentiful with resources, and He will drive out their enemies, but God will not go. It seems as if God can't go because the Israelites are so intent on rebelling, and God is concerned that He will have to destroy them along the way (vv. 3, 5).

When the Israelites hear these words, they humble themselves and mourn. God has them strip themselves of their jewelry, as He determines what to do with them (vv. 5–6). Again, God appears in conflict with himself. He loves these people and longs to be near them. However, He is holy, and they are not; like oil and water, they just don't mix. God doesn't want to destroy the people that He loves. In His compassion, He seeks to constrain himself from judging and puts distance between them. Israel's story is a cautionary tale. God blessed these people beyond measure. Upon their exodus, the Israelites had Egyptian jewelry to wear, enough gold and jewelry to make an idol, and later they will generously contribute their

---

7   Jackie Hill Perry, *Holier Than Thou: How God's Holiness Helps Us Trust Him* (Nashville: B&H Publishing, 2021), 120–21.

gold, ornaments, and fine linens to the building of the tabernacle, and they will still have more to spare. These people had more riches than they knew what to do with. Therefore, you must ponder: What would you do if God blessed you with everything that you want? The word of caution is this: we don't need capital without character.

My husband is a corporate executive. In our conversations, we remind each other of the purpose of our work, and we remember that God is the one who provides for our family. I know the harsh realities of the corporate world, what my husband sees, and the temptations that he faces every day to do what is "normal" to get ahead. So, for many years, I have offered a simple prayer to God on my husband's behalf: "Don't take him anywhere that his character can't keep him." I don't want my husband out here making a lot of money while destroying God's reputation, being an embarrassment to the ministry of our family, or removing the spiritual protections that living a humble and submitted life provides for our daughter. That cost is too high, so I pray.

Israel couldn't handle the blessings that God generously provided for them. They had capital with no discipline, no humility, and no character. They had capital with no real love for God as is evident because their hearts were not submitted to the Lord. So, you want to become a millionaire? For what reason? "What good is it for someone to gain the whole world, yet forfeit their soul?" (Mark 8:36). How are you gonna use the blessings provided to glorify God, and not make idols and altars of worship for yourself? Sometimes the things that we want can destroy us, and that's why God has us wait on them or He puts distance between us and the thing. Every now and again, God gives us an opportunity to invest the generosity of His gifts into His kingdom, and that is what Israel does with the building of the tabernacle. At other times, God sees fit to remove the desired thing from His people altogether.

Follow the Leader

Moses could lead well because he was first a good follower. All great leaders must first learn how to follow. Moses was a submitted follower of Yahweh. He was present, he listened, he was teachable, and he followed the Lord's instructions. "Followship" requires consistency and practice, discipline, and faithfulness. These are the leadership characteristics that we observe in Moses's interactions with God at the tent of meeting. Read Exodus 33:7–10.

Moses was mentoring and leading the people through his actions. Through his submissive posture and humility, the Israelites understood that Moses was not manipulating or forcing them to do his personal bidding. Moses got his instructions directly from the Lord, because "the LORD would speak to Moses face to face, as one speaks to a friend. Then Moses would return to the camp" (v. 11) to deliver God's instructions to the people. And the Israelites were not the only ones watching. Moses had a mentee, Joshua, that humbly submitted to Moses's leadership and served him without wavering.

I have a passion for mentorship and was mentoring the next generation before it was cool. After mentoring peers in my college dorm, leading countless mentoring groups in my home, and starting two mentoring ministries, I started writing articles, speaking, and training others on the topic, and I eventually published my first mentoring book, *Mentor for Life*, and leader's training manual[8] in 2016. Mentoring the next generation of young people within Joshua's age group is different because they are not yet adults. They're "grownish." Moses shows us that mentorship for this age group requires intentional action.

In 2012, I gathered a team of friends who shared my passion for mentoring and commitment to raising up the next generation of leaders. By 2015, we formally established a 501(c)(3) nonprofit, Leadership LINKS,

---

8   The *Mentor for Life Leader's Training Manual* is only available for purchase at Amazon.com.

Inc., where we provide leadership education with character and spiritual development. We actively mentor several young women and men like Joshua. Our commitment to "Mentoring Across Generations" requires that we teach and train the next generation, and that we give them the opportunity to practice followship *before* they lead. Exodus 33:11 reveals how Moses took God's instructions back to the people, but "his young aide Joshua son of Nun did not leave the tent." Joshua is standing watch. Recall how Joshua accepted the opportunity to lead a unit of warriors to defeat the Amalekites (17:8–16). Joshua learned warfare through practice. He followed Moses around as his apprentice and became a teachable student. Joshua proved himself trustworthy even when Moses wasn't around. Eventually, he will become Moses's successor.

Everybody in the next generation wants to lead, but too many are not humble, responsible, teachable, or patient enough to become followers first. The Bible instructs us that we ought not to despise small or humble beginnings because the Lord rejoices at the beginning of a work (Zechariah 4:10). God knows how He plans to equip Joshua for leadership and his work of service, and God knows what the process is going to take. Too often, we are focused on the destination of where we want to go, while ignoring that God rejoices in the process and preparation of our leadership. Joshua continues his leadership training by keeping watch day and night at the tent of meeting, sometimes alone in a hot desert when no one is looking or singing his praises.

When I first joined the military, we had to memorize rates, ranks, and insignia. One of the rates, "11 General Orders of a Sentry," was about keeping watch:

- To walk my post in a military manner, keeping always on the alert, and observing everything that takes place within sight or hearing.
- To report all violations of orders I am instructed to enforce.

- To quit my post only when properly relieved.
- To talk to no one except in the line of duty.
- To give alarm in case of fire or disorder.
- To be especially watchful at night and during the time for challenging, to challenge all persons on or near my post, and to allow no one to pass without proper authority.[9]

Keeping watch is serious business. It requires discipline, showing up on time, and staying the entire time to reinforce these orders and other standards. It is not a time for playing or socializing. There are tasks to complete, rounds to make to ensure that the facility is safe and secure, and that all people and products are in their proper location, doing their assigned work. There are messes to fix and issues to report. There are logs to keep. Standing watch requires integrity. Most of the time, you can't sleep while on watch (certainly not if you are standing watch alone). The watch stander must always be vigilant even at three o'clock in the morning. Standing watch is a test of one's character.

I see too many young people and some adults who want to lead anything, yet these same people cannot consistently complete small tasks with integrity. They want to get paid for ministry but won't consider volunteering. *Why would somebody trust you with leadership that is so sacred when you haven't proven yourself trustworthy in meeting basic ministry needs?* Standing watch is a test of Joshua's resolve. *Are all things going to be orderly and decent when Moses returns, or will Joshua be found asleep?* The Bible says that those who prove themselves faithful over a few things get to expand their leadership (Matthew 25:23). Joshua is going to become a great leader, and his leadership is built on the training grounds of his mentorship as he humbly submits to Moses's leadership and proves himself trustworthy and faithful over his current assignments.

---

9   Recruit Training Command, "11 General Orders of a Sentry," US Navy, accessed December 13, 2021, https://www.bootcamp.navy.mil/general_orders.html.

Exercise

As you reflect on Joshua's leadership, consider the mentors in your life. Take opportunities this week to intentionally thank them. We all benefit from being mentored and by mentoring others. Reflect on your categories from the previous exercise. In what areas can you offer mentorship to others?

Who will you invite into a mentorship relationship? When can you get started? In which categories do you need mentorship? Set an intentional plan and timeline for reaching out to at least three people who can potentially mentor you for where you are in your personal and/or professional journey, and where you would like to go. Maybe you need a mentor to help you through these exercises, or to clarify your next steps. Who will fulfill this role? When will you reach out to them? What will you say when you do?

Leadership and God's Presence

SCRIPTURE READING
Exodus 33:12–34:9

Moses said to the Lord, "You have been telling me, 'Lead these people.' . . . but I don't know what I'm doing. . . . " [Exodus 33:12], but I don't know what I'm doing. Are you gonna offer me some help?" He continues, "If you are pleased with me, teach me your ways so I may know you and continue to find favor with you" (v. 13). Moses is honest, vulnerable, and teachable in the Lord's presence. *New York Times* best-selling author Dr. Brené Brown is the expert on vulnerability. She writes that rising strong requires "the rumble" or owning of our stories, and we can begin that process by asking ourselves three questions:

Category 1: What more do I need to learn and understand about the situation?

Category 2: What more do I need to learn and understand about the other people in the story?

Category 3: What more do I need to learn and understand about myself?[10]

Each of these categories have supporting questions. Category 1: "What do I know objectively? What assumptions am I making?"[11] Category 2: "What additional information do I need? What questions or clarification might help?"[12] Category 3: "What's underneath my response? What am I really feeling? What part did I play?"[13] Answering these questions can help with your exercises, and provide us insight into Moses's understanding of his own leadership story.

Moses is an authentic leader, and we can use Brown's questions to assess his leadership.

> **The situation:** God has called Moses to leadership, but Moses doesn't know how to effectively accomplish the task. That's why he needs God's help and favor.

> **Other people in the story:** Moses understands that the Israelites are God's people (Exodus 33:13). Moses does not have possession over the people that he is called to lead and mentor. He is not their master.

> **Lessons about self:** Moses continues to learn that he and the Israelites need God's presence; an angel isn't good enough and doesn't provide Moses with the confidence needed to continue on the journey (v. 15).

Moses has grown significantly in his leadership from the time that God spoke with him at the burning bush. At the first encounter, Moses wanted

---

10 Brené Brown, *Rising Strong: How the Ability to Reset Transforms the Way We Live, Love, Parent, and Lead* (New York: Random House, 2017), 78–79.
11 Brown, *Rising Strong*, 92.
12 Brown, 93.
13 Brown, 93.

God to send anybody else to accomplish the task (4:1–17). He made all kinds of excuses about why he couldn't (or didn't want to) take on his leadership assignment. Now, he is not trying to quit, even though the task is hard, the road is long, his leadership has been met with much resistance, and he has lost people along the way. His posture has shifted from *if* he can accomplish the leadership task at hand to *how* can he accomplish it.

Moses asks God, "How will anyone know that you are pleased with me and with your people unless you go with us? What else will distinguish me and your people from all the other people on the face of the earth?" (33:16). During the conversation, God replies, "My Presence will go with you, and I will give you rest" (v. 14). He also said to Moses, "I will do the very thing you have asked, because I am pleased with you and I know you by name" (v. 17). Because Moses believes God, he leans in to ask for . . . not more stuff . . . not more favor . . . not an easier journey . . . not more respect or acclaim. Moses asks for more of God himself. "Now show me your glory" (v. 18).

This is a bold ask because Moses has already seen God at work through the bush that burned but was never consumed by the fire. He saw God in the plagues and the miraculous destruction of Egypt. He saw God in their mass exodus, their provision, and God's final blow at the Red Sea. He saw God every time His Spirit descended on the tent of meeting in the form of a cloud and fire speaking to the people, telling them when to move and when to shelter in place. Now he is asking to see God's face, and it is a dangerous request (v. 20). God is a Spirit, so metaphors including parts of the body are sometimes used to communicate personal touch. Moses is asking to experience God's presence in a more intimate way. This is a request that God graciously grants (vv. 19–23).

Then God puts Moses to work chiseling out the stone tablets to replace the first ones that Moses broke (32:15–16). Moses carried those stones up the mountain (34:1–4). "Then the LORD came down in the cloud and stood there with him and proclaimed his name. . . . 'The LORD, the LORD, the compassionate and gracious God, slow to anger, abounding in love and faithfulness, maintaining love to thousands, and forgiving wickedness, rebellion and sin. Yet he does not leave the guilty unpunished; he punishes the children and their children for the sin of the parents to the third and fourth generation" (vv. 5–7).[14] Immediately, Moses bows down to worship (v. 8). Again, he intercedes on behalf of the people, "If I have found favor in your eyes, then let the Lord go with us. Although this is a stiff-necked people, forgive our wickedness and our sin, and take us as your inheritance" (v. 9).

We have had the privilege of listening to intimate conversations and prayers between God and Moses. This is what an authentic relationship with God looks like: it includes prayer, rehearsing God's word back to Him because that shows that we have studied God's way and our hearts are submitted to God, confessing sins, interceding on behalf of others, petitioning God for our needs, being honest, and laying ourselves bare before the Lord. We have seen that Moses's prayers are not self-seeking. He is praying God's best for God's people, and he is doing so using God's own words. As Moses prays and worships in God's presence, he goes without food and water for another forty days (34:28). All alone with God in the wilderness, Moses proves the truth of Jesus's words, "Man shall not live on bread alone, but on every word that comes from the mouth of God" (Matthew 4:4). Moses reveals the heart of a leader that God can use.

Question

How are you currently responding to God's leadership assignments?

---

14 Review our teaching in Exodus 20:5.

The Son Revealed

SCRIPTURE READING
1 Corinthians 10:1–11

SCRIPTURE REVIEW
Exodus 40:34–38

The final verses of Exodus read, "Then the cloud covered the tent of meeting, and the glory of the LORD filled the tabernacle. . . . So the cloud of the LORD was over the tabernacle by day, and fire was in the cloud by night, in the sight of all the Israelites during all their travels" (40:34, 38). Remember that God's presence was symbolized throughout Israel's journey by a cloud and fire, which provided guidance from the moment God first spoke to Moses at the burning bush, and when God separated the Israelites from the Egyptians at the Red Sea (13:21–22).

Now is the time to ask the question, "What does all of this mean for us?" To answer that question, we turn our attention to Paul who wrote that Israel's exodus serves as a teaching tool *and* warning. All Jews who heard Paul's letter would have known the exodus story, and they would have understood that he was challenging them to reflect on it. Paul wrote, "For I do not want you to be ignorant of the fact, brothers and sisters, that *our ancestors [the Israelites] were all under the cloud* and that *they all passed through the sea*. They were all baptized into Moses *in the cloud* and *in the sea*" (1 Corinthians 10:1–2, emphasis added). You might ask, "What does 'being baptized into Moses' mean?"

For starters, "being baptized into Moses" affirms what we already know: the Israelites were followers of Moses. Paul uses this as a foundation to make an analogy: in the same way that the Israelites followed Moses into the Red Sea and just as John's disciples received the baptism of repentance by water,[15] believers are to follow and receive the baptism of the Holy Spirit through Jesus Christ. He wrote that the Israelites were "all baptized into Moses *in* the cloud." In Exodus 40:34–38, the cloud and fire were used as symbols of God's presence and guidance, and throughout Israel's journey as signs of God's protection.[16]

The cloud covered the tabernacle from evening until morning (Numbers 9:15). It determined when the Israelites moved, when they rested and set up camp for the night (vv. 16–21, 23). Sometimes the cloud was over the tabernacle for one night; at other times it loomed for days, a month, or even a year (v. 22). In Numbers 11:25–29, God spoke to Moses out of the cloud and the Spirit of God rested on the elders, giving them the gift of prophesy.

The Holy Spirit is at work and that's why Paul is encouraging followers of the way (Christians) to become baptized into Jesus Christ like the Israelites were baptized *in the sea* with Moses (1 Corinthians 10:2). "Water is a powerful force. It heals and nourishes; it devastates and destroys. It also tells stories of exodus."[17] Water is symbolic of cleaning, new birth, and the work of the Holy Spirit (John 3:1–7). When Jesus told Nicodemus that no one enters the kingdom of God unless they are born of the water and of the Spirit (v. 5), He was making a spiritual claim using physical birth as a metaphor. It is also a metaphor

---

15 Matthew 3:1–11; Mark 1:1–8; and Luke 3:2–18.
16 Exodus 13:21–22; 14:19–20, 24; 16:10; 19:9, 18; 24:15–16; 33:9–10; 34:5; and Numbers 9:15–16; 11:2–3.
17 Kat Armas, *Abuelita Faith: What Women on the Margins Teach Us about Wisdom, Persistence, and Strength* (Grand Rapids, MI: Brazos Press, 2021), 53.

for change, so the "sea" can represent water baptism. When we undergo water baptism, we are professing that the Holy Spirit is at work in us, we are new creatures as a result, and our allegiance has transferred to God's kingdom as we become public witnesses of Jesus. Therefore, Paul was taking his hearers back to the beginning of Israel's journey where they understood the Red Sea as a type of baptism. This vantage point is significant because it gives us an opportunity to do a quick summary and highlight a vital revelation as we close.

The crossing of the Red Sea was a public event (Exodus 14). God was revealing himself, was making a distinction between and sending a message to the Israelites and the Egyptians. "They will *all* know that I am the Lord." Remember how the pillar of cloud moved behind the Israelites to separate them from the Egyptians (v. 20), and how God looked down on the Egyptians from the pillar of fire and cloud. God the Son was at work in the shaming of Pharaoh, and Israel's deliverance. In 1 Corinthians 10:3–4, Paul wrote, "[The Israelites] all ate the same spiritual food and drank the same spiritual drink; for they drank from the spiritual rock that accompanied them, and that rock was Christ." Paul is telling us that the sacrifices, food, and festivities are not the only practices that set Israel apart from Egypt. The Son of God was the rock that accompanied the Israelites on their journey.

Take Heed

Exodus is a case study and warning for the New Testament church (1 Corinthians 10:11). Even with God's presence and the Son as their guide, "God was not pleased with most of them; [and that's why] their bodies were scattered in the wilderness" (v. 5). Pay attention when you read other books of the Torah. Every time you witness large groups of people dying, it is always a result of their sin, over which the holy God must exercise His righteous judgment.

Paul wrote that Exodus serves as an example to "keep us from setting our hearts on evil things as they did" (v. 6). Remember how favorably the Israelites recalled their Egyptian enslavement, revealing their desire to become like the Egyptians? God says: Do not admire or aspire to live like the people of this world![18]

God's people are not to live, dream, or worship like the people who bear allegiance to this fallen world, who have not set their hope on the freedom that God generously offers. Taking the road back to enslavement is taking the road of death. When writing 1 Corinthians 10:7–8, Paul told his hearers again not to follow the sacrilegious festivals which included elaborate meals and sexual debauchery in demonic temples. And he is warning New Testament believers, in effect, "Don't be like the Israelites who were eating from the table that God generously set for them, while still longing to keep the remnants from Satan's table." That is not a sacred baptism! We must reject any unholy alliance. By God's grace and the power of His Holy Spirit that dwells within every believer, He helps us heed Paul's warnings, learn from Israel's example, and put aside the unjust ways of this world.

Questions

Have you experienced God's glory through baptism?

If so, how has that experience changed you?

If not, what interest has this study piqued about baptism?

---

18   Psalm 37:35–40; 73; and Isaiah 58.

God's Divine Power

We close this study by remembering the significant power of the Lord's presence, His faithfulness in keeping Israel, and His power to keep us. We have received an invitation to enter the troubled baptismal waters and cling to the Holy Trinity—considering the faithful promises of our divine Father; the spotless sacrifice of His Son, Jesus; and the dwelling of the Holy Spirit within us—because God is the "divine power [which] has given us everything we need for a godly life through our knowledge of him who called us by his own glory and goodness" (2 Peter 1:3). To Him alone be glory and honor in your tabernacle and throughout the earth, forever and ever. Amen.

We want to see God—to be aware of his presence—but so often we miss him because we are evaluating the wrong things in the wrong way. We try to determine whether God is at work based on our own prosperity and temporal "blessings." However, the Bible has a different standard of evaluation. Through Moses' story we learn that God communes with us in the mountaintop experiences of our lives, but also in the wilderness, on the long walk to freedom, and in the waves of the wild and dangerous waters.

God is with me in the water—to rescue me from all the consuming patterns of thought that remain from a life and history of being enslaved. Let there be no doubt that we have all been enslaved to something. . . .

Get baptized and come out anew. Go into or come out of the troubled waters. That's the invitation from God to each of us. Enter into the pain and suffering of this life to find your purpose and passion through a new life. . . . We have an invitation to lay our pain and burdens down.

Natasha Sistrunk Robinson, *A Sojourner's Truth*

Group Discussion

1. What is your biggest takeaway from this study?

2. What questions do you still have, or will you continue to explore?

3. How does the Trinity make us holy and provide everything that we need on our wilderness journey?

4. How can we encourage each other to continue the journey to freedom?

5. What do you need to remember and reflect on for your present life situation? What will anchor you and give you hope for your future?

Benediction

The LORD bless you and keep you;
the LORD make his face shine on you
and be gracious to you;
the LORD turn his face toward you
and give you peace.

(Numbers 6:24–26)

Amen.

NATASHA SISTRUNK ROBINSON is president of T3 Leadership Solutions, Inc. and visionary founder of the 501(c)(3) nonprofit Leadership LINKS, Inc. A graduate of the United States Naval Academy and Gordon-Conwell Theological Seminary, the doctoral candidate is a sought-after international speaker, leadership coach, and consultant with more than twenty years of leadership experience in the military, federal government, academic, and nonprofit sectors. She is the author of several books including *Voices of Lament*, *A Sojourner's Truth*, and *Mentor for Life*, and she hosts *A Sojourner's Truth* podcast. Natasha has honorably served her country as a Marine Corps officer and employee at the Department of Homeland Security.

Natasha Sistrunk Robinson Ministry: www.natashaSrobinson.com

T3 Leadership Solutions, Inc. www.t3leadershipsolutions.com

Visionary Founder & Chairperson of Leadership LINKS, Inc.
www.leadershiplinksinc.org

Twitter: @asistasjourney

Facebook: www.facebook.com/NatashaSistrunkRobinson

Instagram: @asistasjourney

A Sojourner's Truth podcast www.natashasrobinson.com/podcast

YouTube: www.youtube.com/NatashaSistrunkRobinson